Creating Apps in Kivy

Dusty Phillips

Beijing · Cambridge · Farnham · Köln · Sebastopol · Tokyo

Creating Apps in Kivy

by Dusty Phillips

Copyright © 2014 Dusty Phillips. All rights reserved.

Printed in the United States of America.

Published by O'Reilly Media, Inc., 1005 Gravenstein Highway North, Sebastopol, CA 95472.

O'Reilly books may be purchased for educational, business, or sales promotional use. Online editions are also available for most titles (*http://my.safaribooksonline.com*). For more information, contact our corporate/institutional sales department: 800-998-9938 or *corporate@oreilly.com*.

Editors: Meghan Blanchette and Rachel Roumeliotis	**Indexer:** Judy McConville
Production Editor: Nicole Shelby	**Cover Designer:** Randy Comer
Copyeditor: Rachel Monaghan	**Interior Designer:** David Futato
Proofreader: Rachel Head	**Illustrator:** Rebecca Demarest

April 2014:   First Edition

Revision History for the First Edition:

2014-04-08:   First release

2014-08-22:   Second release

See *http://oreilly.com/catalog/errata.csp?isbn=9781491946671* for release details.

ISBN: 978-1-491-94667-1

[LSI]

Table of Contents

Preface

This book introduces Kivy, an exciting new graphical user interface library that finally allows Python to be used to code cross-platform applications on most traditional and mobile operating systems. I'm happy you're here to study Kivy with me and hope that you'll enjoy reading it as much as I have enjoyed writing it. I am confident that you will be happy with the two Apps you develop and deploy in this book and that it will lead you to develop many new applications of your own design. I look forward to seeing your Kivy Apps on the Android and iTunes market in the near future!

Who Should Read This Book

This book is primarily targeted to fairly new programmers who have read the Python tutorial, but haven't done a lot of real-world coding. In addition to instructing you in Kivy, this book introduces you to the programming workflow. Each chapter builds on the previous chapter to help you create a fully functional mobile application. You will learn the steps you need to follow to design and implement your own apps.

It will also be applicable to programmers who have not worked with Python before but want to use Kivy for its amazing API, integrated multitouch support, or cross-platform deployment. You will probably want to review the Python tutorial to get a leg up on the language's syntax before reading this book. You may be able to skim some sections of the text if you already understand the culture of coding.

Technology Used in This Book

The examples in this book all target Python 3. All but three of them also run seamlessly on Python 2.7. Those three examples have been highlighted in sidebars that include simple workarounds you can use to make the code run on both Python 2.7 and Python 3. Then, any future examples that use the same code will always use the version that works on both Pythons.

I encourage you to use Python 3 if possible, as it is a more enjoyable language to work with, provides nicer APIs, and is slowly being adopted by the entire Python community. That said, depending on what operating system you use, Python 2 may be easier to deploy and develop against at this time. You will have no trouble using Python 2.7 with the examples in this book if you prefer it.

This book was written entirely against Kivy 1.8, which is the first version of Kivy to support Python 3. The examples have been tested somewhat against Kivy 1.7, and it works with all the chapters except Chapter 6. Please use Kivy 1.8 or later if you can. The Kivy developers move very fast, and the newest version is always far better than the previous one in all dimensions: speed, stability, and features.

Conventions Used in This Book

The following typographical conventions are used in this book:

Italic
> Indicates new terms, URLs, email addresses, filenames, and file extensions.

`Constant width`
> Used for program listings, as well as within paragraphs to refer to program elements such as variable or function names, databases, data types, environment variables, statements, and keywords. Also used for commands and command-line options.

`Constant width bold`
> Shows commands or other text that should be typed literally by the user.

`Constant width italic`
> Shows text that should be replaced with user-supplied values or by values determined by context.

 This element signifies a tip or suggestion.

 This element signifies a general note.

This element indicates a warning or caution.

Using Code Examples

Supplemental material (code examples, exercises, etc.) is available for download at *https://github.com/oreillymedia/creating_apps_in_kivy*.

This book is here to help you get your job done. In general, if example code is offered with this book, you may use it in your programs and documentation. You do not need to contact us for permission unless you're reproducing a significant portion of the code. For example, writing a program that uses several chunks of code from this book does not require permission. Selling or distributing a CD-ROM of examples from O'Reilly books does require permission. Answering a question by citing this book and quoting example code does not require permission. Incorporating a significant amount of example code from this book into your product's documentation does require permission.

We appreciate, but do not require, attribution. An attribution usually includes the title, author, publisher, and ISBN. For example: *"Creating Apps in Kivy* by Dusty Phillips (O'Reilly). Copyright 2014 Dusty Phillips, 978-1-491-94667-1."

If you feel your use of code examples falls outside fair use or the permission given above, feel free to contact us at *permissions@oreilly.com*.

Safari® Books Online

 *Safari Books Online* is an on-demand digital library that delivers expert content in both book and video form from the world's leading authors in technology and business.

Technology professionals, software developers, web designers, and business and creative professionals use Safari Books Online as their primary resource for research, problem solving, learning, and certification training.

Safari Books Online offers a range of product mixes and pricing programs for organizations, government agencies, and individuals. Subscribers have access to thousands of books, training videos, and prepublication manuscripts in one fully searchable database from publishers like O'Reilly Media, Prentice Hall Professional, Addison-Wesley Professional, Microsoft Press, Sams, Que, Peachpit Press, Focal Press, Cisco Press, John Wiley & Sons, Syngress, Morgan Kaufmann, IBM Redbooks, Packt, Adobe Press, FT Press, Apress, Manning, New Riders, McGraw-Hill, Jones & Bartlett, Course Technology, and dozens more. For more information about Safari Books Online, please visit us online.

How to Contact Us

Please address comments and questions concerning this book to the publisher:

O'Reilly Media, Inc.
1005 Gravenstein Highway North
Sebastopol, CA 95472
800-998-9938 (in the United States or Canada)
707-829-0515 (international or local)
707-829-0104 (fax)

We have a web page for this book, where we list errata, examples, and any additional information. You can access this page at *http://oreil.ly/apps-kivy*.

To comment or ask technical questions about this book, send email to *bookques tions@oreilly.com*.

For more information about our books, courses, conferences, and news, see our website at *http://www.oreilly.com*.

Find us on Facebook: *http://facebook.com/oreilly*

Follow us on Twitter: *http://twitter.com/oreillymedia*

Watch us on YouTube: *http://www.youtube.com/oreillymedia*

Content Updates

August 2014

Updates to this book include the addition of a new game app in Chapters 10, 11, and 12. These chapters cover advanced graphics, basic game physics, and game design.

Acknowledgments

My editor at O'Reilly, Meghan Blanchette, has been a dream to work with. I've read acknowledgments in many other books in which authors thanked their editors "first and foremost." My experience with other editors has often made me wonder why. Meg's support has been terrific throughout the process of writing this book.

Please heap gratitude on the entire Kivy development team. I've been doing GUI programming for years and have touched many toolkits in Python and other languages. Kivy is the first of the many user interface toolkits I have used that I truly enjoy. Designing a good UI API is extremely challenging (or someone would have got it right before now), and the Kivy developers deserve many, many accolades for their amazing work. Please tip them profusely using Gittip (*http://www.gittip.com*)!

I want to especially thank Gabriel Pettier (tshirtman) not only for developing and maintaining Kivy, but also for his technical review of this book. He pointed out many flaws, omissions, and inconsistencies, which helped me refine the end product into what it is. Jennifer Pierce also tech-reviewed the book from a beginner's perspective and highlighted the areas where I was confusing my readers.

Finally, I want to thank every person who has ever spoken publicly about dealing with mental illness. The wall of silence around all mental illnesses is doing society a huge disservice. Every time someone speaks about this topic, the mentally ill are perceived as somewhat more acceptable and contributing members of society. I've done many incredible things since dealing with a near-terminal form of my illness three years ago. Others have not been so fortunate. We need to talk so that brilliant minds can discover that treatment is available before they succumb to their illness, as Aaron Swartz and Ilya Zhitomirskiy did.

## CHAPTER 1

Introducing Kivy

Kivy is a modern graphical user interface toolkit. It allows you to easily develop natural interfaces for a wide selection of devices. It is attractive to a variety of developers for a few key reasons:

- Kivy has elegant built-in support for multitouch devices.
- Kivy is the only viable way to code in Python on mobile devices.
- Kivy replaces the horrible APIs of earlier graphical interfaces like HTML and CSS.
- Kivy allows you to maintain a single application for numerous operating systems.

Whatever your reasons for studying Kivy, I'm glad you found this book. You'll be going step by step through Kivy basics to create and deploy a fully functional application. Each chapter presents a working program that you will expand on in subsequent chapters. I've chosen to develop a weather application with you, partially because it's at the right complexity level, but mostly because there aren't any decent open source weather applications in the F-Droid open source Android market!

While I hope this book appeals to a diverspe array of developers, I have a specific audience in mind as I write it. As with any job description, you don't have to completely fit this profile, but it will help you to understand who I'm thinking about and how you might differ. My intended audience:

- Has beginner to intermediate programming skills and has read the Python tutorial
- Is not intimately acquainted with advanced Python concepts, but is eager to learn
- Wants to learn about programming workflow, not just Kivy
- Has a good sense of humor
- Owns an Android or iOS device

Regardless of who you are, if you're interested in creating a working application in Kivy, you're in the right place! I'll be showing you how to develop a weather application step by step. You'll start with setting up a Kivy development environment and end up with an application running on your Android device or iPhone.

Dependencies: The Hard Part

It's an unfortunate truth in the programming world that the fun part has to come after a lot of work. Getting Kivy up and running is not a terribly complicated process, but I wouldn't call it enjoyable. "I got a programming library installed after half an hour of effort" just doesn't have the same ring as, "I made a program window pop up after 20 seconds!" So, to boost your excitement, let me tell you that 20 seconds after you get all these dependencies set up, you'll have written and run a small Kivy application. Ready? Let's go!

Python 2 Versus Python 3

There are currently two active versions of Python: Python 2 and Python 3. The syntax and standard library have changed between the two versions, and both are quite popular. You may be wondering which one you should use.

As of version 1.8, which is used for the examples in this book, Kivy supports both Python 2 and Python 3 interpreters. From a developer's point of view, I recommend using Python 3, as it is a simpler syntax, has a cleaner standard library, and will be more useful knowledge going into the future.

However, from an ease-of-use perspective, you are more likely to find that Python 2 is already installed on your computer and ready to go. Further, the tools used to deploy to both Android and iOS currently run only on Python 2.

I wrote the examples in this book to run in Python 3. However, most of them can be run unmodified on Python 2, and I have noted any differences in sidebars.

Regardless of which version of Python you choose, make sure you're using Kivy version 1.8 or later.

Frankly, writing about dependency setup is frustrating for me as well. I don't know what operating system you're using. I don't know what libraries you already have installed or how they conflict with each other. I can't predict the myriad ways that things might go wrong for you.

Luckily, Kivy has great installers for most operating systems. You can use these to get up and running quickly. Quick installers have their downsides, though. A major one is that you, as the developer, don't know exactly what they are doing. This can cause headaches later when things break and you don't know what's going on. However, Kivy takes good care of its users, so it will probably be quite a long time before you have to work out the details.

While I use and recommend the Linux operating system (all the code in this book was first written and tested on Linux), I don't provide Linux installation instructions. Installing dependencies in Linux tends to be much more straightforward than on other operating systems. However, the instructions for doing so vary completely depending on which Linux distribution you are using, and as a Linux user, you probably know better than I how to go about getting them for your distribution of choice (unless you use Arch Linux, for which I've written a ton of documentation). Kivy has terrific instructions for most popular Linux distributions on its downloads page (*http://kivy.org/#download*).

Installing on Mac OS

You can download an all-inclusive *.dmg* file that includes a compiled version of Kivy, all the libraries it depends on, a shell command to run it from a terminal window (this is necessary to see debugging output), and all the examples that Kivy supplies in case you get stuck.

To install it, simply download the latest (version 1.8 or higher) *.dmg* file from Kivy's download page (*http://kivy.org/#download*). Double-click the file in your downloads folder or stack to open it. Then drag and drop the *Kivy.app* file into the *Applications* folder shortcut inside the volume.

Before you close the *.dmg* volume, also double-click the *Make Symlinks* file. This will allow you to run Kivy as a script on the terminal. This script is kind of a wrapper for the Python executable. After you've run `Make Symlinks`, you can open a terminal and type `kivy`. You'll be presented with a standard Python prompt as if you had run the `python` command directly.

In Mac OS Mavericks (10.9), Apple introduced a new antideveloper feature to prevent running "unlicensed" programs. It will pop up a warning that you can't run the script downloaded from the Internet and doesn't provide an obvious way for you to get in on the debate.

There is a hidden workaround, though (I guess Apple just wants you to prove you know what you are doing). In Finder, open the folder containing the script. Then Control-click the icon and click Open in the shortcut menu. This will override the security settings and allow the script to run.

This prompt is your system Python with some paths modified to ensure that all the libraries it requires are installed. If you're an experienced Python coder, you're likely wondering why you wouldn't just use a *virtualenv*. Virtual environments are great when your dependencies are Python libraries that you can install from pypi or Git repositories. However, many of Kivy's dependencies are C libraries that have complicated interdependencies. These have been bundled into *Kivy.app* as a bunch of dynamic libraries that are loaded when you run the `kivy` script.

Note that *Kivy.app* uses the default Python that comes with Mac OS. That means you'll be using Python 2 instead of Python 3. You will have to adapt a couple of the examples in this book to make them work, but I've highlighted those so you won't have any trouble.

For the most part, you will be using Kivy from the terminal in this book. Your file will be named *main.py*. I may tell you to run `python main.py`, but if you're using the Mac OS *Kivy.app*, you'll want to run `kivy main.py` instead.

Installing on Windows

Windows can be pretty quirky for software development. It doesn't have a terrific command-line interface, and there can be bizarre conflicts between software libraries or software and the heterogeneous collection of hardware that Windows supports.

That said, the Kivy developers have done a great job of bundling the dependencies into a single ZIP file. The archive contains the minimum dependencies you need to run Kivy. This portable package should integrate well with the operating system and isolate you from conflicting libraries on the same system.

Download the Kivy for Windows ZIP file from Kivy's download page (*http://kivy.org/#download*). Extract (right-click the file and click "Extract all") the ZIP file to a known directory on your system; I recommend the folder *C:\utils\kivy*.

Now you can open a Windows command prompt. Type the command `cd C:\utils\kivy` and then just `kivy`. This will activate the Kivy environment, which includes the libraries you need. It also bundles a Python executable (you can choose between Python 2 and Python 3 from the downloads page). You will have to perform this activation step each time you open a new terminal.

Note that you can also install msysgit (*http://msysgit.github.io/*) to get a programmer-friendly command-line interface (the same command shell used by default on Linux and Mac OS). If you are using this package, you'll need to run `source kivyenv.sh` instead of the `kivy` script. I recommend using this installer, as you will also have access to the Git version control system to manage your source code, and it will install some of the dependencies you'll need in Chapter 9.

Writing Code: The Easy Part

Now create a directory somewhere to host your project and open a new file called *main.py* in your preferred text editor.

Program Editors

I'm assuming you've done some basic Python development before diving into Kivy. That probably means you've explored the world of Python editors already. All Python programs are simple text that is organized into the structure expected by the Python interpreter. There are numerous tools for editing Python programs, and even more opinions on which one is best.

If you already have such an opinion, then stick with it, by all means. However, if you're feeling confused by the array of program editing choices, I can recommend Sublime Text (*http://www.sublimetext.com/3*). It is very easy for novices, with no more of a learning curve than the basic Microsoft Notepad. However, it is also an advanced editor that professionals, including myself, use for their daily programming. The best part is that if Sublime doesn't do something that you need it to do, you can easily extend it using plug-ins written in Python!

The starting Python module for all Kivy applications should be named *main.py*, as the build tools you'll use later to automate deployment to mobile devices will look for that file. Now add a couple of lines of code to this new file, as shown in Example 1-1.

Example 1-1. The most basic Kivy app

```
from kivy.app import App


App().run()
```

That is it: the most basic Kivy code you could possibly write. It imports an App class, instantiates it, and then calls the run method. Run this code by activating your Kivy environment in a terminal and typing **python main.py** (or **kivy main.py** on Mac OS). It will pop up a blank window with a black background. Close it.

The Kivy App object does an impressive amount of work on your behalf. That is the beauty of object-oriented programming. This object does something, and all you have to do is tell it to do its job by invoking the run method. It takes care of all sorts of stuff: interacting with the screen hardware; talking to input devices such as multitouch displays, keyboards, and accelerometers; scheduling tasks; and more. We'll get into some of that later, but for now, just know that if you don't have an App object, you don't get a window.

If you aren't familiar with the basics of object-oriented programming, you might want to review the relevant section of the Python Tutorial (*http://bit.ly/py-classes*). If you'd like in-depth coverage of the topic, see my book *Python 3 Object Oriented Programming* (Packt, 2010).

In Kivy, your use of object-oriented principles is largely to extend Kivy's built-in objects through inheritance. This is a fairly easy paradigm to understand, so you don't need to be well versed in classes to get there.

If a blank window with a black background is exactly the kind of application you were looking to write, then you're done! Congratulations. Perhaps you can skip to the chapter on deploying so you can get that black background onto your mobile device (or just use the power button; black goes with anything).

Personally, I'd like something a little more interesting. So let's try again. Edit the file to look like Example 1-2.

Example 1-2. A slightly less basic Kivy app

```
from kivy.app import App


class WeatherApp(App):
    pass

if __name__ == '__main__':
        WeatherApp().run()
```

This version uses inheritance to create a new subclass of `App` called `WeatherApp`. This is the application you'll be developing in this book. You didn't actually add anything to the new class, so it behaves exactly the same as the previous version. However, you'll be extending it a lot in subsequent chapters. It also wraps the call to `App.run` in an `if` statement to make sure that this file can be imported from inside other files later in the book. More importantly, you can now use the KV language to add some real user interface elements to that black window.

Introducing the KV Language

The KV language, often referred to as *kvlang*, is a simple markup syntax that I think of as "what HTML would look like if HTML looked like Python." It's a very clean syntax and makes Kivy interface design much more enjoyable than any other toolkit I've worked with, including the Web.,

You'll be creating a new file to store the KV language in. Call it *weather.kv* and save it in the same directory as *main.py*. Your *.kv* file should always have the same name as your app class, but with the word `App` stripped from the end, and converted to lowercase. Thus, `WeatherApp` will always look for its layout information in a file called *weather.kv*.

I'll be explaining more about the KV language throughout the book. Start by putting Example 1-3 in your *weather.kv* file.

Example 1-3. Simple KV language file

```
Label:
    text: "Hello World"
```

This is a very simple KV language file that creates a new `Label` object and sets its text to the infamous `Hello World` string. If you now run the `python main.py` command, you will see the window pop up, still with a black background, but also with the text displayed in its center, as shown in Figure 1-1.

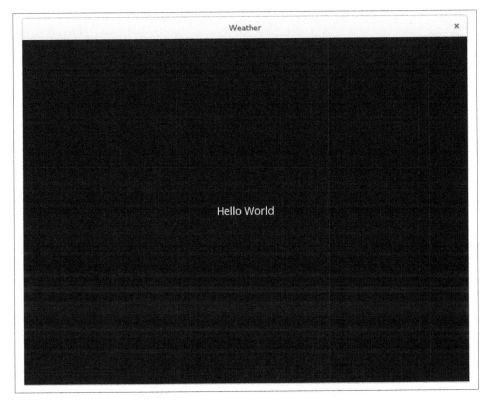

Figure 1-1. Hello World label

User Interface Design

Each chapter in this book builds on the results of the chapter preceding it. At the end of the book, you will have created a weather application that runs on your desktop computer, Android, and iOS. It's a good idea, before you write an application, to know what kind of application you want to write. Therefore, let's spend a few minutes discussing what features the app will support and how it will look.

Weather apps tend to have the same set of features. Here are some capabilities I want to cover in this project:

- Render weather for multiple locations, with a selector to switch between them.
- Store the list of locations between App invocations so they don't have to be searched again.
- Switch between current conditions and long-term forecast.
- Include settings for users to choose metric or imperial units.
- Incorporate gestures for users to switch between screens.

Given these features, it's fairly easy to imagine the set of views the application will require:

- A form for adding new locations
- A list of previously searched locations
- The current conditions screen
- The forecast screen
- The settings screen

These will, of course, be composed of other interface components. I'll introduce the widgets you require as they come up. The remainder of this chapter will focus on the form for adding a new location. This form is pretty simple, requiring only a text entry field in which to type a city name, and a button to search for that location (see Figure 1-2 for a mockup).

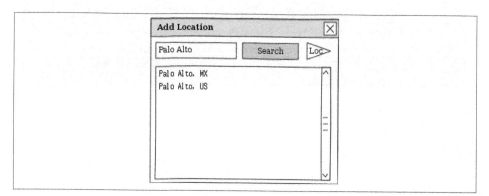

Figure 1-2. Mockup of Add Location form

I'll also add a button to search for the current location, assuming the device has a GPS. Finally, there needs to be a list of results so users can choose which of multiple matching cities is the one they want.

Mockups

Mockups are an essential component of user interface design. They give quick insights into how to lay out visual application components. Normally, the first mockup you create will indicate flaws in the design (especially if you show it to an experienced user interface designer… or your client) that you can address before putting any effort into actually coding an inappropriate interface.

I personally tend to do my mockups using a pencil and plain paper. One of my far too many hobbies is sketching, and paper puts me into a more creative frame of mind than the computer screen, which I spend too much time staring at as it is.

However, my sketches are not professional enough to show to clients (or render in a book). There are plenty of online and desktop applications for creating mockups. I enjoyed the closed source Balsamiq (*http://balsamiq.com/*) when my company provided a license for it. I am loath to pay for software, though, so the mockups in this book were all done using the open source Pencil (*http://pencil.evolus.vn/*).

Whatever you choose, you should have, at the very least, a mental picture of what you want your interface to look like. The KV language is awesome for implementation and prototyping, but for the initial design phase, you'll want more freedom and feedback.

Widgets

Kivy uses the word *widget* to describe any user interface element. Just a few examples of widgets include:

- The label you rendered in Example 1-3
- The text input field and buttons you'll render shortly
- Layout classes that comprise other widgets and determine where they should be displayed
- Complicated tree views such as file pickers
- Movie and photo renderers
- Tabbed boxes that display different widgets depending on the selected tab

I find it convenient to think of a widget as a sort of box that has behaviors and can contain other boxes. The Widget class is the most basic such box. It is empty. However, all other widgets extend this class in a beautiful inheritance hierarchy. The Label widget is a very simple widget that displays text. The Button widget is more interactive and responds to touch or click events. The TextInput widget knows how to deal with keyboard events.

The more advanced widgets, such as TabbedPanel or FileChooser, are composed of multiple other widgets. There is really no conceptual difference between an advanced and a primitive widget other than the difficulty of drawing them on the screen. Advanced widgets are normally composed of Layout widgets, which are essentially boxes that know enough about the widgets inside them to determine how they should be sized and positioned relative to one another. There are several different Layout subclasses. I personally use BoxLayout unless I have very specific needs that require a GridLayout or FloatLayout. BoxLayout, which renders widgets in a vertical or horizontal line, tends to be better suited to adapting its size to the display on which it is currently rendering.

Finally, you can make custom widgets of your own by extending the Widget class (or, often, a Layout subclass) and applying KV language rules to describe how the widget should look. There are two ways to do this. One is to create custom drawing commands to render graphics directly to the widget canvas. The other is to compose multiple primitive widgets into something more complicated; that's what you'll be doing in this chapter.

The KV Language Root Widget

The KV language is a special domain-specific language that is ideal for laying out user interfaces. It has a Pythonesque syntax and borrows heavily from Python's notions of simplicity and elegance. The KV language file uses indentation to indicate which "boxes" go inside other boxes.

The outermost box in a KV language file is called the *root widget*. There can only be one root widget per KV language file. In Example 1-3, there was only one widget, a Label, and it is the root widget. You can tell it is the root widget because it is the leftmost indented line, and doesn't have any funny brackets or angle brackets around it to indicate that it is something else.

There is an indented block below the root widget's Label: specifier. Inside this block, you can define other child widgets (except Label doesn't typically have children), and you can specify properties about that widget. I'll tell you more about properties in Chapter 2, including how to create your own custom properties on custom widgets. For now, understand that the Label widget has a text property. That property takes a string value. Like a string value in Python, it is embedded in quotes. A colon separates the property name from the value, much like a key/value specifier in a Python dictionary.

You've probably guessed that the root widget is attached directly to the Kivy window and rendered. If it were a container widget that held multiple child widgets, it would render them as well. Try changing your *weather.kv* file to look like Example 1-4.

Example 1-4. Basic container widget

```
BoxLayout:
    Label:
        text: "Hello"
    Label:
        text: "Beautiful"
    Label:
        text: "World"
```

The root widget, in this case, is a `BoxLayout` object. As I mentioned before, `Layout` widgets are essentially containers that know how to hold other widgets and position them in some way. There are three labels supplied, indented, as children of the `BoxLay out`. Each of these `Labels` has an indented block of its own where that widget's properties are configured; in this example, a different value for `text` is supplied for each.

KV Syntax Errors

If your KV language file doesn't compile correctly, you'll get a Python traceback. Debugging syntax errors is a common task in programming, as it is rare to type code correctly the first time. You will probably even make mistakes and omissions as you type the examples from this book.

The KV parser will typically give you a `ParseException` if it encounters a line it doesn't like. It will mention the line number in the KV language file that is at fault and normally includes a short description of what's wrong in the file.

You will eventually encounter these regularly (at least, if you type like I do). I suggest you force one now so you know what to look for. Try deleting the colon after `text` in one of the labels in Example 1-4 and see what happens when you try to run the app.

By default, the `BoxLayout` places each of its child widgets side by side, from left to right, giving each one an equal amount of space. Since you haven't done anything to change the defaults, this is what happens when you render the KV file. If you now run `python main.py`, it will render three labels, as shown in Figure 1-3.

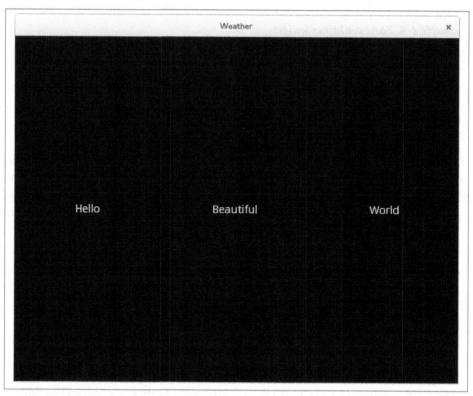

Figure 1-3. Rendering of basic container widget

Creating a Custom Widget

It would not be difficult to change the labels in the root widget to some buttons and text boxes to create the Add Location form I have in mind. But that would make things rather complicated later, when you need to remove all those widgets from the view to put other data (for example, a forecast) on display. Further, if the user later wanted to add another location, it would be tricky to restore all the Add Location widgets.

Instead, create a custom `AddLocationForm` widget that encapsulates the text entry, search button, location button, and search results into a single widget. Then set the root widget to be an instance of that custom widget instead. Example 1-5 does all of this.

Example 1-5. Custom AddLocationForm widget

```
AddLocationForm:  # ❶

<AddLocationForm@BoxLayout>:  # ❷
    orientation: "vertical"  # ❸
    BoxLayout:
        TextInput:
```

```
    Button:
        text: "Search"
    Button:
        text: "Current Location"
ListView:
    item_strings: ["Palo Alto, MX", "Palo Alto, US"]  # ❹
```

❶   The root widget is now a custom widget named AddLocationForm. It doesn't
    have an indented block below it, so there are no properties or child widgets
    defined.

❷   The new custom class is defined here. The @ symbol in the KV language indicates
    that the class is extending BoxLayout using inheritance. This means that the new
    widget is a BoxLayout and can do all the things a BoxLayout can do, such as lay
    out its children. The angle brackets tell the KV language that this is a new class
    rule, not a root widget.

❸   AddLocationForm is a BoxLayout like in the previous example, but you are setting
    its orientation property to vertical. This will force its child elements to appear
    one above the other. The child elements in this case are another BoxLayout (this
    one is horizontal), and a ListView.

❹   I'll tell you a lot more about the ListView widget later. For now, because search
    isn't implemented yet, just hardcode a couple of values so you can see what the
    rendered ListView looks like.

The rendering of this code is shown in Figure 1-4. It's already looking a lot like I want
it to look, but the widget proportions are all wonky.

Adjusting Widget Size

There are a couple of proportion problems with the rendering in Figure 1-4. First, the
text box and two buttons are way too tall. And second, the text box doesn't take enough
of the available width. This is fairly easy to take care of in terms of lines of code. However,
I find setting proportions on Kivy widgets to be confusing. I hope to spare you that
frustration by giving a thorough explanation in this section!

It is up to the Layout object to determine what size its child widgets should be. It is
allowed to take two types of advice from its children, should the children choose to
provide it, but it is also free to ignore that advice. For example, a horizontal BoxLay
out will always make its children the same height as itself, no matter what the child
requests (this can cause extensive problems if the child widget is in its teens).

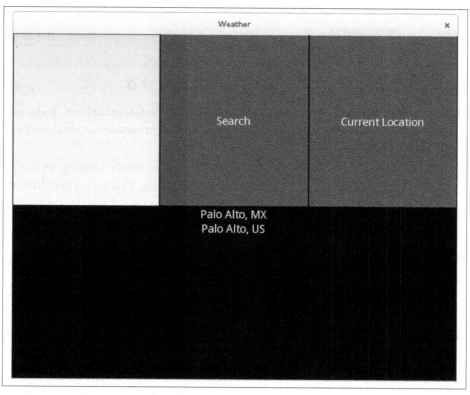

Figure 1-4. Rendering of AddLocationForm

The two types of advice the child can give its parent layout are size hints and absolute sizes. For each type of advice, the child widget can set properties in the x dimension (horizontally) and the y dimension (vertically). In addition, it is possible to combine the horizontal and vertical settings in the case where you need to explicitly set both of them. This is unecessary with BoxLayout, since it always uses maximum space in one direction, but can be useful with other layouts. Thus, there are technically six different proportion advice properties that you can set on any given widget class:

- size_hint_x
- size_hint_y
- size_hint (tuple of size_hint_x, size_hint_y)
- width
- height
- size (tuple of width, height)

Of course, if you use the tuple version, you shouldn't use the individual dimension version.

Size hint advice

The size_hint is a proportional measure. If three widgets have the same size_hint (and the layout chooses not to ignore that information), they will all be the same size. If one widget's size_hint is twice as big as another widget's, then it will be rendered at double the size.

The main thing to bear in mind is that the size of a widget is calculated based on the sum of the size_hint values for all the widgets. A single widget having a size_hint of 1 has no meaning unless you also know that its sibling widget has a size_hint of 2 (the first widget will be smaller than the second) or 0.5 (the first widget will be larger). Have a look at Example 1-6, rendered in Figure 1-5.

Example 1-6. Size hints

```
BoxLayout:
    orientation: "vertical"
    BoxLayout:
        Button:
            size_hint_x: 1
        Button:
            size_hint_x: 1
        Button:
            size_hint_x: 1
    BoxLayout:
        Button:
            size_hint_x: 1
        Button:
            size_hint_x: 2
        Button:
            size_hint_x: 3
    BoxLayout:
        Button:
            size_hint_x: 1
        Button:
            size_hint_x: 0.75
        Button:
            size_hint_x: 0.25
```

The first button in each row has a size_hint_x value of 1. However, its size is different in each row because the sibling buttons in each row have size_hint_x values that are bigger or smaller.

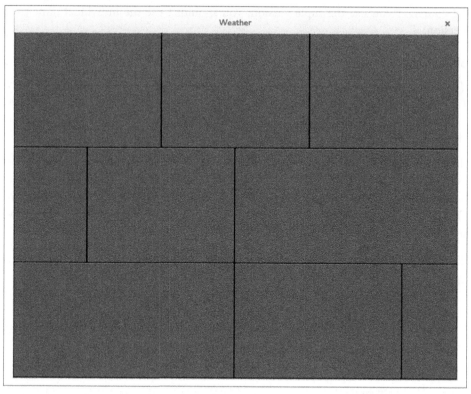

Figure 1-5. Size hints

Size advice

Sometimes having widget sizes calculated relative to the sizes of other widgets is exactly what you need. Other times, you need to control the size in one or both dimensions a little more accurately. This is where the width and height properties come in.

 One of the most frustrating layout issues for Kivy newbies is that size properties (including width and height) are ignored unless the relevant size_hint properties are set to None. The default value for a size_hint is 1.0.

Thus, as a rule of thumb, any time you choose to set a height on a widget, you must also set size_hint_y to None. Similarly, any time you set a width, you must set size_hint_x to None if you want to get the expected results. And, of course, if you set the size property instead, you should set size_hint to (None, None).

The `width` and `height` values themselves are pretty easy to interpret. They can be integer values, in which case they refer to the pixel size of the widget on the screen. However, you can also pass string values such as `"1cm"`, `"0.75in"`, or `"100dp"` to render the widget relative to the resolution of the display. This is almost always a good idea, because modern devices can have an extremely wide variety of pixel densities. A pixel on a cheap laptop might be three times the size of a pixel on a high-end smartphone, and the disparity is even larger for so-called retina displays.

Personally, unless I have a good reason to do otherwise, I always use Kivy's concept of *display pixels* by passing a suffix of `dp` to my `height` and `width` properties. A display pixel is a resolution-independent value that roughly maps to "the size of a pixel on a typical laptop at 72 dots per inch." On a lower-end screen, 1 display pixel is equivalent to 1 pixel. On top-end displays, a display pixel might be 3 or 4 real pixels wide. The display pixel will be roughly the same size on all the devices; it's the pixels themselves that are smaller. It's not guaranteed, but I find that a display pixel on mobile devices is a bit bigger than on desktops and laptops. This is useful, since touch interfaces need to provide a bit more room for widgets to accommodate the clumsy size of the human finger.

Remember that a given layout is free to ignore the `width` and `height` properties if it so chooses. Also remember that most `Layout`s will ignore those properties no matter what, if the `size_hint` has not been set to `None` in that dimension. Keep this knowledge close to hand, and you should (I hope) never have to go through the trauma that I did to figure out Kivy sizing! It's really quite elegant; I don't know why I once found it so difficult.

See it in action

After all that reading, you're probably eager to see some KV language code. Hopefully Example 1-7 will satisfy you.

Example 1-7. Setting widget sizes on AddLocationForm

```
AddLocationForm:

<AddLocationForm@BoxLayout>:
    orientation: "vertical"
    BoxLayout:
        height: "40dp"  # ❶
        size_hint_y: None
        TextInput:
            size_hint_x: 50  # ❷
        Button:
            text: "Search"
            size_hint_x: 25  # ❸
        Button:
            text: "Current Location"
            size_hint_x: 25  # ❹
```

```
ListView:  # ❺
    item_strings: ["Palo Alto, MX", "Palo Alto, US"]
```

❶ Pay close attention to the indentation so you can tell what size property has been set on which widget. Remember, there are two BoxLayout objects. The outer AddLocationForm, a type of BoxLayout, is vertical. You are setting the inner (by default, horizontal) BoxLayout to have an explicit height of 40 display pixels. This means the TextInput and two button widgets inside will be constrained to that height, since they expand to fill the full height of the parent. Note the explicit setting of size_hint_y to None!

❷ The TextInput is given a size_hint_x of 50 to make it take up half the width of the window, since the parent widget takes up the full window size.

❸ ❹ The two Button objects are assigned a size_hint_x of 25 so they each take up a quarter of the width. The size_hint_x values for the three widgets total 100, making it easy for us to think of them as percentages.

❺ The ListView has not been given any additional size information. Its size_hint defaults to (1, 1). It's in a vertical BoxLayout, so its width will be the full width of the parent. The only other widget in that BoxLayout has a size_hint_y of None, so the ListView will take up all remaining vertical space after the 40dp for the other BoxLayout is deducted.

The result is rendered in Figure 1-6. It was clearly coded by a programmer, not a user interaction designer, but it does the job and beautifully illustrates the concepts you've learned in this chapter.

File It All Away

Programming is a task that is best learned by doing, not reading, studying, watching, or listening. Take some time to try things and mess up. I close each chapter with a set of explorations you can use to guide your study. Don't think of them as exercises. Think of them as topics. Programming is best facilitated by a sense of wonder. Never be afraid to ask, "What happens if I do this?" (unless you are testing on live code deployed to a nuclear facility, moving vehicle, or my personal mobile phone). Here are a few ideas to get you started:

• Check out Kivy's extensive API documentation (*http://bit.ly/kivy-api*), focusing on the kivy.uix modules, which describe the widgets shipped with Kivy. Pay special attention to the different types of Layout classes. BoxLayout is usually the best choice unless you're doing something specific.

• Clone the Kivy repository and check out the *examples* directory. Pay particular attention to the *showcase* and *kivycatalog* examples in the *demo* folder. The latter even allows you to interactively change KV language code to see what happens. It's pretty awesome (I wrote it).

- Try coming up with several toy layout projects using the widgets you encountered in this chapter and any others that tickle your fancy. If you're having trouble coming up with ideas, try a basic login form (TextInput has a Boolean password property) or a web browser toolbar.

- Experiment *a lot* with different size_hint and size combinations on a BoxLay out until you understand what works and what doesn't.

- Experiment with the other built-in Layout classes that come with Kivy. FloatLay out and GridLayout are popular for certain specific tasks. AnchorLayout and StackLayout have, in my opinion, less common utility. Figure out how each interprets size_hint and size.

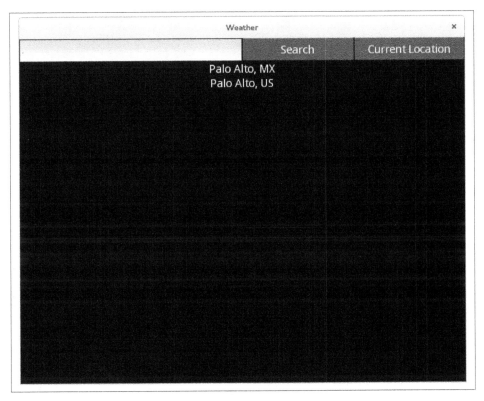

Figure 1-6. AddLocationForm with reasonable widget proportions

## CHAPTER 2

Events and Properties

In this chapter, you'll learn what Kivy means, specifically, by the words *event* and *property*. You'll also learn how to respond to events using event handlers and how changing properties automatically fires events on those properties. I'll include a digression on choosing client libraries. By the end of the chapter, you will be able to search for weather locations anywhere in the world.

What Is an Event?

Dictionary.com defines an event as "something that happens, especially something important." That's a perfect description of events in Kivy. Kivy is firing events all the time, but you only have to pay attention to those that you consider important. Every graphical toolkit has some concept of events. The difference between Kivy and those other toolkits is that in Kivy, event dispatch and handling are sane and uncomplicated.

Like most user interface toolkits, Kivy provides an *event loop*. This is executed by your Python code when you call the run method on WeatherApp. Underneath the hood, this method is constantly cycling through events such as touch or mouse motion, clock ticks, keyboard entry, accelerometer input, and more. When something interesting happens, it does the necessary processing to make sure that your code knows the event has happened and has a chance to respond.

So if an event is something that happens, an event handler is something that responds to something that happens. In Kivy, an event handler is just a function or method. By the end of this chapter, your event handler is going to search for potential locations to retrieve weather for and add them to the ListView. But you can start a bit smaller: how about just printing a message to the console from which your Kivy app is running?

Adding Logic to a Custom Widget

I have a guideline. It's a strict guideline—you might call it a rule—but there are legitimate reasons to break it. The guideline is this: layout and graphical information should always go in the KV language file. Logic (the calculations and activities that make up a program) should always go in a Python file. Keeping these two types of information separate will save hours in the long-term maintenance of your app.

You may have noticed in the previous chapter that I didn't touch the Python file at all. All the changes happened in the KV language file. This is because that chapter was entirely related to the user interface. This chapter is going to do some logic. Granted, that logic is going to change the user interface (for example, by updating the values in the ListView), but such activity still belongs in the Python file.

The Python file, therefore, needs to know about the AddLocationForm custom widget that you defined in Chapter 1. I kind of cheated in that chapter by allowing the KV language file to create a class dynamically using the @BoxLayout syntax. Take that out first, as shown in Example 2-1.

Example 2-1. Making AddLocationForm into a normal, rather than dynamic, class

```
AddLocationForm:

<AddLocationForm>:  # ❶
    orientation: "vertical"
    BoxLayout:
        height: "40dp"
        size_hint_y: None
        TextInput:
            size_hint_x: 50
        Button:
            text: "Search"
            size_hint_x: 25
        Button:
            text: "Current Location"
            size_hint_x: 25
    ListView:
        item_strings: ["Palo Alto, MX", "Palo Alto, US"]
```

❶ The @BoxLayout was removed, changing this into a normal class.

You won't be able to run this KV language file because you took out the Kivy magic that allows it to know what kind of class it's supposed to be. Dynamic classes are a shortcut in Kivy that are most often useful if you want to reuse the same widget layout settings —without logic—in multiple locations. For example, if you had a group of buttons that all needed to be styled similarly, you could create a dynamic class that extends @But ton and set the relevant properties on them. Then you could use instances of that class in multiple locations, instead of having a bunch of duplicate code for all the buttons.

However, `AddLocationForm` is a rather normal class that needs logic attached to it. Start by adding a class definition to the *main.py* file, as shown in Example 2-2.

Example 2-2. Adding a class to main.py

```
from kivy.app import App
from kivy.uix.boxlayout import BoxLayout   # ❶


class AddLocationForm(BoxLayout):   # ❷
    pass


class WeatherApp(App):
    pass

if __name__ == '__main__':
        WeatherApp().run()
```

❶ Remember to import the class you are extending.

❷ Inheritance is used to create a new subclass of `BoxLayout` with no extra logic just yet. The rule in the KV language file, which matches this class based on the class name, will apply all the additional styling for this form. This styled class is then set as the root class in the KV language file.

If you now run `python main.py`, it will behave exactly the same as at the end of Chapter 1. Not much gain, since all you've done is make the code more verbose, but you'll be adding logic to this class right away.

Responding to Events

Quickly add a method to the new class that prints a short maxim to the console when it is called, as shown in Example 2-3.

Example 2-3. Adding some very simple logic

```
class AddLocationForm(BoxLayout):
    def search_location(self):   ❶
        print("Explicit is better than implicit.")
```

❶ The method doesn't accept any arguments. This is just a normal method; it's not an event handler.

You'll be adding an event handler to the KV language file now. It's just one line of code. The boundary between user interface and logic should, in my opinion, always be one line of code in the KV language file. That single line of code can, and should, call a method in the Python file that does as much processing as is required. Have a look at the modified code for the search button in Example 2-4.

Example 2-4. Hooking up the event handler

```
Button:
    text: "Search"
    size_hint_x: 25
    on_press: root.search_location()   ❶
```

❶ The event handler is accessed as a property on the Button object with a prefix of on_. There are specific types of events for different widgets; for a button, the press event is kicked off by a mouse press or touch event. When the press event happens, the code following the colon—in this case, root.search_location() —is executed *as regular Python code.*

When you run this code, you should see the phrase Explicit is better than im plicit display in the console every time you press the Search button in the interface. But what is actually happening?

When the press event fires, it triggers the event handler, which is essentially just a method on the Button class named on_press. Then it executes the contents of that method, which has been defined in the KV language file to contain the single line of code root.search_location().

Assume, for a second, that the root variable points at an instance of the class that is leftmost indented in this KV language block—that is to say, the <AddLocationForm> class rule. This object has a search_location method, since you added it just a few moments ago, and that method is being called. So, each time you touch the button, the print statement inside search_location is executed.

In fact, that assumption is correct. When the KV language executes anything as raw Python code, as in these event handlers, it makes a few "magic" variables available. You just saw root in action; it refers to the leftmost indented object: the current class rule. The self variable refers to the rightmost indented object. If you accessed the self.size property from inside the on_press handler, you'd know how big the button was. Finally, the app variable refers to the subclass of App on which your code originally called the run method. In this code, it would be an instance of WeatherApp. This isn't that useful in your current code, but when you start adding methods to WeatherApp, the app magic variable will be the way to access them.

Accessing Properties of KV Language Widgets

Before you can search for the value that the user entered into the text box, you'll need to be able to access that value from inside the Python code. To do that, you need to give the widget in question an identifier, and then provide a way for the Python file to access that named object.

This is a good time to delve into the Kivy concept of *properties*. Kivy properties are somewhat magical beings. At their most basic, they are special objects that can be attached to widgets in the Python code and have their values accessed and set in the KV language file. But they add a few special features.

First, Kivy properties have type-checking features. You can always be sure that a `String` property does not have an integer value, for example. You can also do additional validation, like ensuring that a number is within a specific range.

More interestingly, Kivy properties can automatically fire events when their values change. This can be incredibly useful, as you will see in later chapters. It's also possible to link the value of one property directly to the value of another property. Thus, when the bound property changes, the linked property's value can be updated to some value calculated from the former.

Finally, Kivy properties contain all sorts of knowledge that is very useful when you're interfacing between the KV language layout file and the actual Python program.

For now, just know that the `ObjectProperty` property can be bound to any Python object. Your KV language file will be set up to attach this property to the `TextInput` object. First, though, set up your *main.py* code to import `ObjectProperty` and add an instance of it with an empty value to `AddLocationForm`, as shown in Example 2-5.

Example 2-5. Adding a property to point at the search input widget

```
from kivy.properties import ObjectProperty   ❶


class AddLocationForm(BoxLayout):
    search_input = ObjectProperty()   ❷

    def search_location(self):
        print("Explicit is better than Implicit")
```

❶   Remember to import the class.

❷   The property is created at the class level as an instance of the `ObjectProperty` class.

Next, modify the *weather.kv* file to do two things. First, you want to give the `TextIn put` an `id` property so that it can be internally referenced from other parts of the KV language file. Note that these `ids` aren't useful outside of the KV language rules. That means you'll also have to set the value of the `search_input` property you just created to this `id`. The KV language will take care of setting the value in your Python code to point directly at the `TextInput` widget object. Make the two modifications shown in Example 2-6.

Example 2-6. Setting the search input id and property value

```
AddLocationForm:

<AddLocationForm>:
    orientation: "vertical"
    search_input: search_box   # ❶
    BoxLayout:
        height: "40dp"
        size_hint_y: None
        TextInput:
            id: search_box   # ❷
            size_hint_x: 50
        Button:
            text: "Search"
            size_hint_x: 25
            on_press: root.search_location()
        Button:
            text: "Current Location"
            size_hint_x: 25
    ListView:
        item_strings: ["Palo Alto, MX", "Palo Alto, US"]
```

❷ First, add an `id` attribute to the `TextInput` so it can be referenced by name elsewhere in the KV language file.

❶ Then set the value of the property, which was defined in Example 2-5, to that `id`.

The Difference Between Kivy Properties and Python Properties

Kivy and the Python language both have concepts they call *properties*. In both cases, properties sort of represent named values on objects, but they are not the same thing, and you have to be careful to distinguish between them. They are not interchangeable at all. In the context of Kivy development, Kivy properties are more useful, but there is nothing stopping you from using Python properties as well, for other purposes.

A Python property is a method (or set of methods) that can be accessed as if it were an attribute. Different methods are called if the property is retrieved or set. This can be a useful form of encapsulation.

Kivy properties, on the other hand, are not a language feature, but are simply objects that wrap a bunch of logic for the various features described in the text. They are specified on widget classes, and the Kivy internals know how to seamlessly map them to each instance of those properties as used in the Python code or KV language file.

Kivy will take care of making sure that the `ObjectProperty` in the Python code directly references the `TextInput` widget object, with all the properties and methods that the `TextInput` has. Specifically, you can now access the value the user entered from inside the `search_location` method using the `text` property, as shown in Example 2-7.

Example 2-7. Accessing a widget attribute via ObjectProperty

```
def search_location(self):
    print("The user searched for '{}'".format(self.search_input.text))    ❶
```

❶ Access the `text` property on the `search_input` widget. In this example, just print it out.

Populating the Search Result List

Now that you can access the value the user searched for, the next step is to look up possible matching cities. To do this, you need weather data to query.

One option, of course, would be to invest millions of dollars into setting up weather stations across the world; then you'd have your own private network of data to query. Unfortunately, that's slightly outside the scope of this book. Instead, you can take advantage of other services that have already done this part and have made their data publicly available.

I had a look around the vast reserves of the Internet and discovered Open Weather Map (*http://openweathermap.org/api*), which supplies an international API for looking up weather data. I don't know how accurate it is, but this is what you'll be using to create your Kivy interface. It is free, allows essentially unlimited requests, and doesn't require an API key (though it is recommended for production systems). It's also founded on "open" principles like Wikipedia, OpenStreetMaps, Creative Commons, Open Source, and Gittip. I believe strongly in these principles.

Choosing APIs and Libraries

I just arbitrarily told you what API you are going to use to access weather data. This took a huge amount of effort out of the programming process for you. This is unfortunate, as determining what libraries to base your program on is a major part of the development effort. Programming books tend to introduce the subject as if you will be writing all of your work from scratch. This isn't true. The success of any new application is strongly impacted by what third-party libraries or APIs are used to create it. I spend a vast amount of time up front researching available options and trying to figure out which one will maximize the effectiveness of my app.

For any given problem that you need to solve, search the Web to see what existing libraries are available. Programmers hate duplicating work, and you'll find most tasks have already been completed! Once you have a list of available libraries, study each one, paying attention to questions such as these:

- Is the license compatible with the license you want to use for your application?
- If not open source, how much does it cost to license the library?
- If open source, does the source code for the library look well maintained and easy to read?
- Does the library appear to be actively developed and has there been a recent release?
- Is there an active user community talking about the library?
- Does the library appear to have useful (readable, up-to-date, complete) documentation?
- What avenues of support are available if you have trouble?
- If Python-based, does the library boast Python 3 support?

Open Weather Map is a web service that returns data in JavaScript Object Notation (JSON). Python has a superb built-in JSON parsing library that converts the incoming data to Python dictionaries and lists. However, you still need a way to retrieve that incoming data. There are built-in tools to handle this in the Python standard library, but you're much better off using the `UrlRequest` class that Kivy provides. This class supplies a fully asynchronous API, which means that you can initiate a request and allow the user interface to keep running while you wait for a response.

Since this book is about Kivy, I'm not going to give you a lot of detail about the structure of the Open Weather Map data. Its website explains this in detail. The examples include all the code you'll need to actually perform these tasks.

The next step is to connect to the weather map service when the user clicks the Search button and retrieve a list of cities that match those search results. This is not a difficult task. First import `UrlRequest` as shown in Example 2-8 and request the URL as illustrated in Example 2-9.

Example 2-8. Import UrlRequest

```
from kivy.network.urlrequest import UrlRequest
```

Example 2-9. Retrieving map data using requests and printing the list of cities to the console

```
def search_location(self):
    search_template = "http://api.openweathermap.org/data/2.5/" +
        "find?q={}&type=like"    ❶
    search_url = search_template.format(self.search_input.text)
    request = UrlRequest(search_url, self.found_location)    ❷
```

```
def found_location(self, request, data):   ❸
    cities = ["{} ({})".format(d['name'], d['sys']['country'])
        for d in data['list']]   ❹
    print("\n".join(cities))
```

❶   The {} in the URL is a placeholder for the user's query. The str.format method is used in the next line to replace this value with the value that the user actually searched for.

❷   You'll need from kivy.network.urlrequest import UrlRequest at the top of the file. This line is doing a lot of work on your behalf. It connects to the Open Weather Map URL and downloads the response. It then returns control to the UI, but when the response comes back from the network, it will call the found_location method, which is passed in as an argument.

❸   The data passed by UrlRequest is a parsed dictionary of JSON code.

❹   This list comprehension is also doing a huge amount of work. This command is iterating over one list and translating it into a different list, where the elements are in the same order but contain different data. The data, in this case, is a string with the name of the city and the country in which it's located.

 There is a bug in Kivy 1.8.0 under Python 3. When you are using Kivy 1.8.0 and Python 3, UrlRequest fails to convert the incoming data to JSON. If you are using this combination, you'll need to add import json and put data = json.loads(data.decode()) at the top of found_location.

Comprehensions

Comprehensions can be pretty incomprehensible to the uninitiated (and are therefore poorly named). However, they are one of Python's strongest language features, in my opinion. Newer Python users tend to overlook them, so I thought I'd give you a crash course here.

Python has built-in support for *iterators*; that is, container items that can have their elements looped over one by one. Built-in iterators include lists, tuples, strings, dictionaries, sets, and generators. It's trivial to extend these objects or create new objects that can be iterated over. The for loop is the traditional method of iteration.

However, one of the most common tasks of a for loop is to convert a sequence of objects into another, transformed sequence. Comprehensions allow us to do this in a compact and easy-to-read syntax. The transformations that can happen inside a comprehension include:

- Changing the container to a different type of sequence. For example, you can iterate over a set and store the results in a list or dictionary.

- Altering each value into a different format. For example, you can convert a list of strings containing numbers into a list of integers, or you can convert a list of strings into a list of strings with newlines on the end.

- Filtering out values that don't conform to a specific condition. For example, you can convert a list of integers into a list of only the even integers in the list, or you can convert a list of strings into a list of nonempty strings.

You'll see examples of comprehensions throughout this book, but if you want more information, search the Web for *list comprehensions*, *dictionary comprehensions*, or *set comprehensions in Python*.

Now all you need to do is figure out how to update the list of results on the screen instead of printing to the console. This is also surprisingly simple since the data is stored in a Kivy property on the `ListView` widget.

First, add an `id` to the `ListView` and set it up as an assigned property in the *weather.kv* file, as shown in Example 2-10.

Example 2-10. Updating search results

```
AddLocationForm:

<AddLocationForm>:
    orientation: "vertical"
    search_input: search_box
    search_results: search_results_list  # ❶
    BoxLayout:
        height: "40dp"
        size_hint_y: None
        TextInput:
            id: search_box
            size_hint_x: 50
        Button:
            text: "Search"
            size_hint_x: 25
            on_press: root.search_location()
        Button:
            text: "Current Location"
            size_hint_x: 25
    ListView:
        id: search_results_list  # ❷
        item_strings: []  # ❸
```

❶ You don't have an `ObjectProperty` in *main.py* yet, but assign it here anyway.

❷ Set an `id` on the `ListView` so it can be referenced in the property assignment above.

❸ Empty the default values from the list, since you won't be needing them for layout testing anymore.

Then, add the `search_results` `ObjectProperty` to the `AddLocationForm` class and update the contents of the property in the `found_location` method instead of printing results to the screen, as shown in Example 2-11.

Example 2-11. Updating the list of search results on search click

```
def found_location(self, request, data):
    data = json.loads(data.decode()) if not isinstance(data, dict) else data  ❶
    cities = ["{} ({})".format(d['name'], d['sys']['country'])
        for d in data['list']]
    self.search_results.item_strings = cities  ❷
```

❶ Work around the aforementioned bug in which `UrlRequest` doesn't parse JSON under Python 3. This line of code works on both Python 2 and Python 3 and should also work with future versions of Kivy that fix the bug. It is an ugly workaround, but at least the ugliness is constrained to one line. This line uses Python's ternary operator to check if the data has been converted to a `dict` already, and if not, it loads it using the JSON module. You'll need to add an `import json` at the top of the file.

❷ End the chapter with the easiest line of code imaginable: set the `item_strings` property on the `self.search_results` list to the list of cities.

And that's it. If you now run `python main.py`, you can search for Vancouver and get two expected results, as shown in Figure 2-1.

 When you test this search form, you can crash the application by searching for a place with no matches. Search for a real place. You'll explore error checking in the exercises.

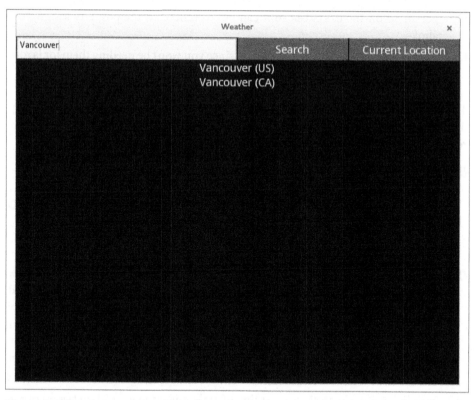

Figure 2-1. Rendering of search results in the basic container widget

File It All Away

We covered two important Kivy topics in this chapter: events and properties. I didn't get into a great deal of detail about either of them yet. You might want to try some of the following tasks to enhance and lock in your new knowledge:

- Accessing the GPS device in Android is covered in Chapter 9, but for now, you could invite users to enter a `latitude,longitude` pair into the text field. If they click the Current Location button, it could signify that they intended to search by latitude and longitude instead of city name. If you look at the documentation for the Open Weather Map database, you can see that it allows searching by latitude and longitude. Try hooking up this button.

- This app crashes if your search doesn't have any matches. I had a great internal debate about this, but I have left error checking out of most of the examples to make sure the code you see is comprehensible. However, that makes the code unrealistic. All real-world code needs to have solid error checking. Try to make the `search_lo cation` and `found_location` methods resilient against searching for places that don't exist, transient network failures, and as many other problems as you can come up with.

- You've only seen the on_press event for buttons. See if you can figure out how to make on_enter on the TextInput object call the same function and perform a similar search.

- Read through the Kivy documentation for some of the basic widgets you've heard about to see what kinds of properties and events are supported for each.

- Try making a new toy app that links the text of a label to the text of an input, such that typing into the input changes the label. Hint: this is easier than you might guess and does not require setting up an on_text handler. It can be done with just a boilerplate *main.py* file; all the connections can happen in the KV language.

## CHAPTER 3

Manipulating Widgets

It's time to think about widgets again. In this chapter, you'll see how to dynamically change what widgets are displayed in the widget tree. You'll mainly be implementing searching and the rendering of search results. This will give you a good understanding of the intricacies of the Kivy `ListView` widget and its adapters, and you'll also learn how to create widgets and update the display dynamically in response to user or system events.

A More Extensible Root Widget

While the user will find it useful for the Add Location form to be rendered the first time the application is run, it's not actually appropriate to set it as the root widget on the app. It's better to have a custom root widget that knows how to manage the widgets that are displayed on it, such as the various forms I mentioned in Chapter 1.

I expect the root widget to have several methods for manipulating the display of child widgets. Start by adding an empty class to the *main.py* file. Make it extend `BoxLayout`, but for now, the class can be otherwise empty (meaning it will behave exactly like a normal `BoxLayout`). See Example 3-1.

Example 3-1. Empty root class

```
class WeatherRoot(BoxLayout):
    pass
```

For now, set up the KV language file to render an instance of this as the root widget. Then set up a new rule for it to include `AddLocationForm` as a child, as demonstrated in Example 3-2.

Example 3-2. Root widget with AddLocationForm child

```
WeatherRoot:

<WeatherRoot>:
    AddLocationForm
```

Since the parent class is a `BoxLayout` with only one child, it will render `AddLocation Form` as taking up 100% of its surface area. So, running the application looks exactly the same as before.

You'll be adding some code to customize this widget class shortly, and a lot more throughout this book, but for now, this empty class is sufficient while you work out how to handle events on the `ListView` object.

ListView Adapters

The Kivy `ListView` API includes full support for managing and displaying selection. However, for starters, all you need it to do is hold a list of widgets that can respond to touch events. When the user touches a location in the Add Location list, you need to respond to the event appropriately. We'll deal with "appropriately" later; for now, just worry about responding to the event!

By default, the `ListView` renders a `Label` widget for each string in the list, but `Label` is an inert widget that doesn't care when it gets touched. Luckily, `ListView` can use different classes (including custom classes) as the widget to be displayed for each item. Kivy supplies two classes, `ListItemLabel` and `ListItemButton`, that behave like normal `Label` and `Button` objects but also contain information for tracking selection. Tracking selection is mandatory for `ListView` widgets, so it's almost always a good idea to extend one of these classes, depending on whether you want to just display data (use `ListI temLabel`) or respond to touch events (use `ListItemButton`).

Start by editing the *weather.kv* file. You'll need to add a couple of `import` statements at the top of the file first, as shown in Example 3-3.

Example 3-3. Imports for adapter buttons

```
#: import ListItemButton kivy.uix.listview.ListItemButton
#: import ListAdapter kivy.adapters.listadapter.ListAdapter
```

KV imports work similarly to Python imports but use a different syntax. They exist because sometimes you need access to Python modules in your KV language file other than those that are magically available as part of the Kivy builder process. This normally happens in the small parts of the KV language file that map to actual Python execution.

Imports in the KV language start with the characters `#: import` followed by an alias for the module or member being imported. This is followed by the full path to the module or class to be imported. The alias can then be used throughout the KV file as a reference to that item. In this case, you need to import `ListAdapter` and the `ListItem Button` classes. See Example 3-4 to learn why.

Example 3-4. ListView with adapter specified

```
ListView:
    id: search_results_list
    adapter:
        ListAdapter(data=[], cls=ListItemButton)
```

It's hard to see the boundary between the KV language and Python here. The adapter property is KV language, but its value is Python code in which you are constructing a `ListAdapter` object. The `ListItemButton` class is then passed into this initializer.

The main thing you need to know about the `ListAdapter` class is that it sits between the `ListView` and the data (in this case, a list of strings). It can do a few things while it's sitting there, like keeping track of which item is selected, making sure the view stays up-to-date when data changes, setting what widget class is used to render the data, and mapping data between the input format and widget properties.

The defaults for all of these settings work fine in this example, except the widget class, which is now set to a `ListItemButton` object instead of the default `ListItemLabel`. Unfortunately, running this code would break the interface because the Python code you wrote previously is not updating the new `ListAdapter`. It's still trying to update the default class on a `ListView`, called a `SimpleListAdapter`. This is easily remedied, as shown in Example 3-5.

Example 3-5. Using the ListAdapter API in the search method

```
def search_location(self):
    search_template = "http://api.openweathermap.org/data/2.5/" +
        "find?q={}&type=like"
    search_url = search_template.format(self.search_input.text)
    request = UrlRequest(search_url, self.found_location)

def found_location(self, request, data):
    data = json.loads(data.decode()) if not isinstance(data, dict) else data
    cities = ["{} ({})".format(d['name'], d['sys']['country'])
        for d in data['list']]
    self.search_results.item_strings = cities
    self.search_results.adapter.data.clear()          ❶
    self.search_results.adapter.data.extend(cities)    ❷
    self.search_results._trigger_reset_populate()       ❸
```

❶   You can't just set the data to an empty list because the container involved is an instance of `ObservableList`. Instead, clear the list...

❷   ...and then extend it with the new data.

❸ ListAdapter is supposed to update the display when it sees the data change, but it's not doing its job, so you should force an update here. This is an undocumented method that it took me half an hour of searching through Kivy source code to find. Sometimes searching through source code is the best way to learn things. The Kivy sources are well written and easy to read; you can learn a ton from perusing them.

Now run the application and search for a location. The ListView renders buttons now, instead of the default labels, as shown in Figure 3-1.

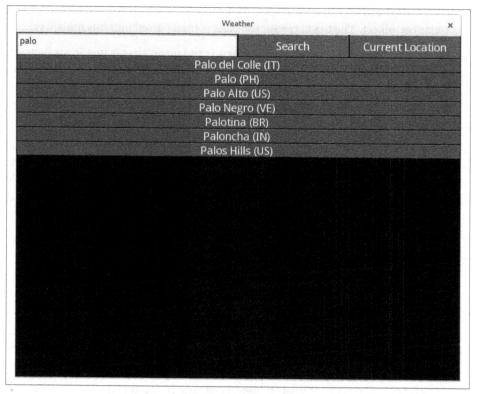

Figure 3-1. Rendering of buttons in the ListView

list.clear in Python 2 and Python 3

The list class, from which Kivy's ObservableList inherits, has a handy clear method. This method is being called in Example 3-5 to remove any previous search results from the list.

Unfortunately, clear was introduced to the list class in Python 3 and isn't available in Python 2. The syntax you'll want to use instead is del self.search_results.adapter.data[:], which effectively deletes all the objects in the list.

Note that you do *not* want to do something like self.search_results.adapter.data = []. This will have the effect of clearing the list, but you will have set the value to a normal list instead of the ObservableList that Kivy originally instantiated on the adapter. This means it won't be able to do the extra Kivy stuff (like listen for change events on the list), and the ListView will be broken.

Responding to ListView Item Events

Unfortunately, these buttons don't provide easy access to event handlers. You can remedy this by making a subclass of the ListItemButton in *main.py*, as shown in Example 3-6.

Example 3-6. Creating a subclass of ListItemButton

```
from kivy.uix.listview import ListItemButton


class LocationButton(ListItemButton):
    pass
```

Next, update the imports in *weather.kv* to import this main module instead of the ListItemButton class; see Example 3-7.

Example 3-7. Importing a custom class from main

```
#: import main main
#: import ListAdapter kivy.adapters.listadapter.ListAdapter
```

Finally, update the cls reference, as shown in Example 3-8.

Example 3-8. Point cls at the new class

```
    ListView:
        id: search_results_list
        adapter:
            ListAdapter(data=[], cls=main.LocationButton)
```

With this slight modification, running the app won't look any different. However, you can now add style rules to the KV language file, including the event handler in Example 3-9.

Example 3-9. KV rule for Location button

```
<LocationButton>:
    on_press: app.root.show_current_weather(self.text)
```

In the KV language, the app magic variable points at the currently running App subclass. In your code, this is an instance of WeatherApp. The App class has a root variable that points at the root object defined in the KV language file—in this case, a WeatherRoot instance. That widget doesn't currently have a show_current_weather function, but you can add that next, as shown in Example 3-10.

Example 3-10. Placeholder to show weather

```
class WeatherRoot(BoxLayout):
    def show_current_weather(self, location):
        from kivy.uix.label import Label
        self.clear_widgets()
        self.add_widget(Label(text=location))
```

 Be careful not to confuse the root magic variable, which refers to the leftmost rule in the current indentation block, with app.root, which always refers to the root widget of the app. app.root refers to the same object anywhere in the KV language file, but root refers to a different thing depending on what rule it is found in.

This method is really just stubbed out as a placeholder. It creates a label in Python code, something you haven't seen before. So far, you've created all your widgets in the KV language file. Occasionally, you need to do it in Python. No widgets accept positional arguments upon construction, but some allow you to pass arbitrary properties into the constructor. Thus, you can set the orientation on a BoxLayout or the size_hint_x on a widget directly when constructing it in Python. This works fine, but it's less readable than the KV language and, more importantly, fails to separate interface concerns from logic.

I imported the Label class directly in the method because this is temporary code that I expect to remove soon. It is a good idea, when coding, to create something that works in as few lines of code as possible and test that before going on. This approach is far easier to debug and far more likely to generate comprehensible code with fewer errors than writing a hundred lines of code and hoping it's correct. I make this point because I want it to be clear that this style of development is valuable, and Example 3-10 is not just a pedagogical example. See it running in Figure 3-2. Note that you'll have to exit the program after selecting the location; you'll be making the AddLocationForm reusable shortly.

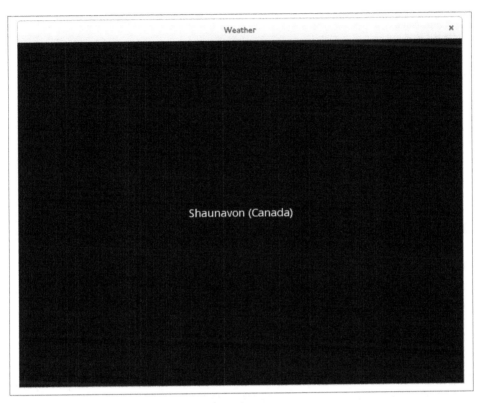

Figure 3-2. Label rendered after selecting a location

Swappable Widgets

You can probably guess that adding a Label directly to the root window isn't going to be a viable long-term solution. What you need is a way to switch between the AddLoca tionForm and the CurrentWeather widget. I'll go through the steps to do this, but take a moment to think about the problem first. How would you approach it?

I think it's pretty clear that another widget is required to hold the "current weather" data. Anytime you add a new widget to your Kivy project, you should ask yourself, "Does this widget need to have a class in the Python code, or can I use a dynamic widget?" Cur rentWeather is largely going to be a display-only object, so a dynamic class seems sufficient for now. The entire widget is stubbed out in Example 3-11.

Example 3-11. Basic layout for CurrentWeather widget

```
<CurrentWeather@BoxLayout>:
    location: ""  ❶
    conditions: None
    temp: None
    temp_min: None
    temp_max: None
    orientation: "vertical" ❷
    Label:
        text: root.location  ❸
    BoxLayout:
        orientation: "horizontal"
        size_hint_y: None    ❹
        height: "40dp"
        Button:
            text: "Add Location"
        Button:
            text: "Forecast"
```

❶ These are the custom properties that I expect to set later when actually setting the weather.

❷ Setting inherited properties on dynamic classes is also allowed. This widget extends BoxLayout, but you want it to render vertically.

❸ The root variable is referencing the CurrentWeather object itself. You're connecting the text property on the Label to the location property that was defined earlier. These are connected dynamically, such that updating the location field on the class will automatically update the displayed label text.

❹ There's a good chance you've already forgotten that you must explicitly set size_hint_y to None if you are setting a height.

Now all you have to do is generate this class instead of a label in *main.py*. Since you're constructing a dynamic class, you won't be able to simply import it. Instead, add the Factory import to the top of the file, as shown in Example 3-12.

Example 3-12. Importing Factory

```
from kivy.factory import Factory
```

Then adapt the show_current_weather method to construct an instance of this dynamic class from the factory, set the location, and render it. Example 3-13 reveals all.

Example 3-13. Constructing a dynamic widget from Factory

```
class WeatherRoot(BoxLayout):
    def show_current_weather(self, location):
        self.clear_widgets()
        current_weather = Factory.CurrentWeather()
```

```
        current_weather.location = location
        self.add_widget(current_weather)
```

Notice how the dynamic class is constructed by the factory. Then it can be treated like any other widget, because it is one. If you run the app and render it, it will look like Figure 3-3.

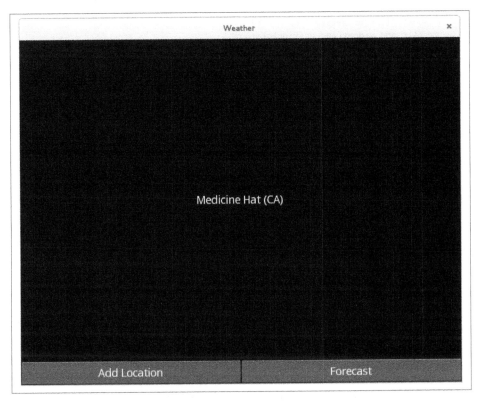

Figure 3-3. Making the widget dynamic

Switching Forms

Try hooking up the on_press handler on the Add Location button that is part of the CurrentWeather widget. It should be a very similar workflow to what you just saw in the previous section, except that instead of constructing a CurrentWeather widget, you'll construct an Add Location form.

Work on this on your own for a bit before looking at the minor changes in Example 3-14 and Example 3-15.

Example 3-14. Event handler for the Add Location button

```
Button:
    text: "Add Location"
    on_press: app.root.show_add_location_form()
```

Example 3-15. New event handling method on the WeatherRoot object

```
def show_add_location_form(self):
    self.clear_widgets()
    self.add_widget(AddLocationForm())
```

Your user can now move back and forth between the AddLocationForm view and the CurrentWeather view. You aren't rendering any real data yet, and the "Add" is a bit of a lie, since all you're doing is switching between locations, not adding them to a list. However, there's some structure coming to the application, and you can see that it will be pretty easy to hook up weather retrieval machinery in the next chapter.

File It All Away

In this chapter, you picked up some additional experience with Kivy properties and events. These concepts are central to any Kivy application. You also learned more details about the complex ListView API and how to manipulate the widget tree. Here are some additional explorations for you:

- Change the background color of the LocationButton. You'll need to check the Kivy docs to find what property to change and how to represent colors in Kivy.

- Rendering the Add Location form every time is unnecessary. Try storing the entire widget as an ObjectProperty on WeatherRoot and add it to or remove it from the view as needed.

- Play with the layout of the Current Weather form to render some more placeholders (Label is sufficient) for Current Temp, High/Low, and Current Conditions.

- If you're looking for something a little more intense, you now have enough knowledge to make a basic to-do list application in Kivy.

## CHAPTER 4

Iterative Development

For the most part, I have been designing the weather app you are now building exactly as I would have designed it without you along for the ride. I am a firm believer in *iterative development*. The basic principle of iterative development is to perform small design changes, one step at a time, such that at the end of each step, you have a working application. It may not be complete in terms of the design requirements, but it is complete in terms of the current version of itself.

Each chapter in this book is a development iteration. This is convenient for me, as an author, because it gives me an end game to focus on for each chapter. However, this is just a lucky coincidence. I hope that you will follow a similar iterative process in developing your own Kivy applications. Indeed, if you really want your iterations to make sense, I advise that your version-control commit messages tell a story, much like this book.

Iterative development is indoctrinated in various formal methodologies of software development. These are useful when you are coordinating development teams, as the more developers a project has, the more communication overhead there is.

If you're working in a team environment (and you will be, at some point), you might want to search the Web for terms such as *extreme programming* or *Scrum*. However, if you're developing mobile Kivy applications by yourself, you can probably get away with informal iterations and a notebook of ideas.

It's impossible to complete everything a project needs in a single development sprint. Therefore, you have to focus on the tasks you want to get done and organize the things that are being set aside. While each iteration is different, I find there are two broad categories:

- New feature development, where one or two major features are added in a single sprint. At the end of the iteration, the features will be working and functional, though they may not be complete.
- Code cleanup, where minor tweaks are made to a variety of previously implemented features to take it from a working demo to a usable product.

This chapter is going to be one of the latter type. You'll learn a few new Kivy principles while solidifying your knowledge of the topics we've already covered. At the end of it, you'll have a functional program that actually renders weather information. It might not be ready for consumption by the general public, but it will work!

Improving the Add Location Form

It would be handy for the search box text input to be automatically focused when the Add Location form is displayed. We can easily accomplish this using the `focus` property on the `TextInput` widget.

You can also hook up the widget such that an Enter keypress fires the search, by using the `on_text_validate` event. However, that event fires only if the `TextInput` has had multiline mode disabled (since the Enter key would insert a line break in multiline mode). For this particular `TextInput`, multiline mode doesn't make sense anyway.

The best part is that this change only has to be made in the *weather.kv* file, as the Python code was designed with the reusable `search_location` method. You can borrow this method in the `on_text_validate` event handler, and the form will respond exactly as though the Search button had been clicked.

These two properties, along with the new `focus` property, are displayed in Example 4-1.

Example 4-1. Three new properties on TextInput

```
TextInput:
    id: search_box
    size_hint_x: 50
    focus: True
    multiline: False
    on_text_validate: root.search_location()
```

If you run the app now, it will look the same, but you'll notice that it is much less painful to interact with. This is a big usability win for three lines of code!

Caching Widgets

Once created, widgets don't always have to be descended from the root window. Obviously, if they are not, they won't be visible on the screen. For example, when the user switches from the CurrentWeather to the Forecast view and back, it probably makes sense to place the same widget back on the screen, rather than hitting the network and rendering the data all over again.

This chapter doesn't feature a Forecast view just yet, but in preparation for it, add to AddLocationForm a cached property and a Cancel button that switches back to the previous location when clicked. Most of this work can happen in the show_cur rent_weather method, as shown in Example 4-2.

Example 4-2. Caching the CurrentWeather widget

```
current_weather = ObjectProperty()    ❶

def show_current_weather(self, location=None):    ❷
    self.clear_widgets()

    if location is None and self.current_weather is None:    ❸
        location = "New York (US)"
    if location is not None:    ❹
        self.current_weather = Factory.CurrentWeather()
        self.current_weather.location = location
    self.add_widget(self.current_weather)    ❺
```

❶   Create an ObjectProperty on the class to store the widget in.

❷   Add a default value to the location parameter so that API users (including your future self) know that None is an option and will check the method contents to see what happens.

❸   A rather ugly special case: if both location and self.current_weather are None, hardcode a default location. This method is typically called in one of two ways. In the first, a location is passed in, because the user just searched for a new location. In that case, the first conditional is skipped, and a whole new self.cur rent_weather widget is constructed in the second conditional. The second way is to pass None into the method, which indicates that the user clicked Cancel on the Add Location form. In this case, both if statements are bypassed and the self.current_weather that was previously displayed is shown once again. The special case happens if there is no self.current_weather widget because the user pressed Cancel the very first time the form was shown. Then the first conditional triggers, and it replaces the None value with a hardcoded location as if the user had actually searched for New York.

❹   If the location is not None, either because it was passed in explicitly or hardcoded above, construct a new CurrentWeather widget. Immediately cache its value inside the ObjectProperty.

❺   Regardless of whether the cached widget was constructed from scratch or previously stored, add it back into the window.

There are two so-called *code smells* in this function. The first is the hardcoded value for location. This is going to cause grief later if you change the format of the location; this hardcoded value won't be in the new format and will have to be updated separately.

The second is the special case on location. If location is None, the method is supposed to render the previously rendered widget. However, the special case occurs if there is no previously rendered widget. Your code has to either explicitly check for this special case, as in Example 4-2, or ensure that the case never occurs. I mention two options for exploring this in the exercises for this chapter.

This isn't a horrible amount of code, but it's about as much code as I ever want to write without testing that it's working properly. To test it, add the Cancel button to the *weather.kv* file, being sure to call the show_current_weather method in its on_press handler. Place the button at the same indentation level as the ListView so it takes up the full width of the screen. You can probably figure this one out on your own by now to confirm; have a look at Example 4-3.

Example 4-3. Adding a Cancel button to the Add Location form

```
Button:
    height: "40dp"
    size_hint_y: None
    text: "Cancel"
    on_press: app.root.show_current_weather(None)
```

Running this code changes the form slightly to look like Figure 4-1.

You should test all three branches through this code. If you run the program and immediately click Cancel, it should render the location as New York (US). If you click Add Location, do a search, and select a different city, it should render that city. Click Add Location once again followed by Cancel to see that the previously selected city still works.

Figure 4-1. Adding a Cancel button to the Add Location form

Storing Actual Locations and Converting Arguments

The Open Weather Map (*http://openweathermap.org*) API expects the city and country name to be specified in a comma-separated list. However, so far, I have combined it into a somewhat more human-readable city (CC) format, where CC is the country code. (I'm not sure what Open Weather Map does if more than one city in a country has the same name!) Take a few minutes to think of some ways to solve this code design issue.

Off the top of my head, I can think of three possible solutions:

- Use regular expression matching to split the city and country back into their component parts. This would probably work flawlessly, but it makes me a bit nervous in case there is some bizarre city out there that has brackets in its name or something.

- Change the format stored in the string to a city,CC value so it can be submitted directly to Open Weather Map. This would also work all right, but would it not be overly readable for the user and would eventually break when Open Weather Map changes its API.

- Store the city and country as a tuple of values so that their structure can be derived and rendered independently. This is probably best for long-term maintenance and will help avoid surprises or difficulty in the future.

The ListAdapter API allows you to separate data from representation of the data. Since you're already using a ListAdapter, you can easily change the representation of the cities assignment in the found_location function to store a list of tuples instead of a list of formatted strings. See Example 4-4.

Example 4-4. Cities as a list of tuples

```
cities = [(d['name'], d['sys']['country']) for d in data['list']]
```

 If you read the documentation for the ListView API, you will discover that there is also a DictAdapter class that allows you to store data in a dictionary instead of a list. This API requires you to maintain both a dictionary and a list of the dictionary's keys (to provide ordering) inside the adapter.

I personally recommend never using this API. Find a way to change your data so that the ListAdapter API works instead. Some options include keeping a separate dictionary and storing only the keys in the ListAdapter, or making the ListAdapter store tuples of (key, value) pairs or, possibly, a list of dictionaries.

After you change the strings to tuples, though, if you run the app, it will break. The default behavior of ListAdapter is to assume it is storing a list of strings and set the text property on whatever display class is being used (LocationButton, in this case) to whatever value that is. Trying to set the text property to a tuple causes Kivy to crash.

So, you need a way to convert the data from a list of tuples to a set of property associations on the LocationButton. Kivy does this very Pythonically, by assigning a custom function called args_converter. This function should accept two values: the index of the item being rendered, and the item itself. Kivy will call this function repeatedly for each item in the underlying data list. This allows you to store the data in whatever format makes sense for your application's underlying data model, and then to convert it to the format that makes sense for your widget's UI only when it is time to invite the UI to render it. Kivy takes care of all of this internally; all you really need to know is that your args_converter takes an item from the data list as input and outputs a dictionary. The keys in this dictionary are any properties (including custom properties) that can be set on the item being rendered (LocationButton). The values are, of course, the values to set for those properties. Example 4-5 summarizes the new method added to the AddLocationForm class.

```
    self.current_weather.update_weather()
    self.add_widget(self.current_weather)
```

The final step is to update the *weather.kv* file to reference the new properties. You can lay this out however you like. I suggest doing some sketches on paper or in a mockup app before you actually start laying things out. The KV language is very easy to work with and can be useful for mocking out interfaces. However, if you don't actually draw it out on paper, you might end up doing what I did and forget to include the current temperature! My mockup looks like Figure 4-2.

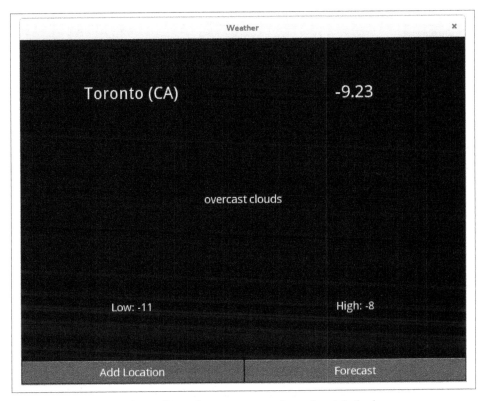

Figure 4-2. Quick mockup of how the current weather tab might look

I didn't mimic this exactly in my code, as displayed in Example 4-17, but I did get all the elements in place.

Example 4-17. Laying out some weather information

```
<CurrentWeather>:
    orientation: "vertical"
    BoxLayout:
        Label:
```

```
                text: "{} ({})".format(root.location[0], root.location[1])
                font_size: "30dp"
            Label:
                text: "{}".format(root.temp)
                font_size: "30dp"
        Label:
            text: root.conditions
        BoxLayout:
            orientation: "horizontal"
            Label:
                text: "Low: {}".format(root.temp_min)
            Label:
                text: "High: {}".format(root.temp_max)
        BoxLayout:
            orientation: "horizontal"
            size_hint_y: None
            height: "40dp"
            Button:
                text: "Add Location"
                on_press: app.root.show_add_location_form()
            Button:
                text: "Forecast"
```

Now you can run the app to check the weather for some common cities. Figure 4-3 shows that it is somewhat chilly in Toronto today.

File It All Away

In this chapter, you iterated on your previous work. You refactored your code into a more maintainable codebase. While you didn't add too much new functionality, aside from actually looking up the current conditions and temperature, you made huge strides. Your future work will go much more quickly because of the changes you made here.

You might want to explore some additional refactorings or new features. Here are some suggestions:

- Don't render the Cancel button on the Add Location form on the initial run of the application. This should reduce the need for the special case in show_cur rent_weather.

- While the search request is being performed, clear any previous search results. This will be important if you do a search and then search for a different location without selecting anything in the result list.

- If you're feeling particularly adventurous, render a pop-up while the search is being performed. As it is, the interface provides no indication that the network request occurred. This is barely noticeable on a Silicon Valley Internet connection, but on a cellular network in the desert it's going to be a frustrating wait to answer the question, "How damn hot is it, anyway?"

- See if you can use the `index` parameter to the `args_converter` method to alternate the background color of individual `LocationButtons`.

- The code now has two functions that construct a URL from a template string and request data from that URL. Perhaps these lines of code should be refactored into a module-level function. Duplicate code is a bad thing. Don't repeat yourself.

- For clarity, I didn't do any error checking on either of those requests. This is fatal in production, because the Internet *never* stays on all the time. Handling errors in Kivy can be ugly, not because the API is bad, but because there are so many decisions that need to be made, and many of them involve the user. You'll need to learn how to do this if you want to release your apps in the wild.

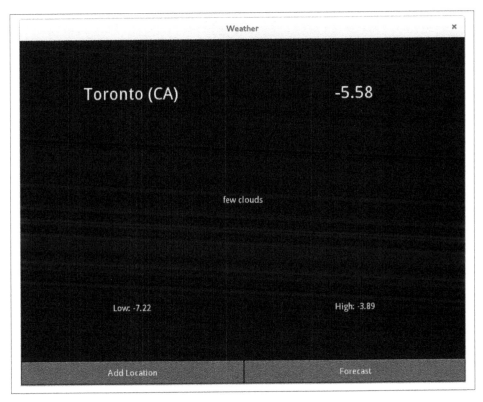

Figure 4-3. The CurrentWeather view

## CHAPTER 5

Kivy Graphics

Kivy provides sophisticated graphics capabilities using OpenGL and SDL instructions. These can be useful if you're creating an interactive game rather than an application with widgets.

In this chapter, you'll learn the basics of the Kivy canvas and graphics primitives. You'll be creating a set of icons (some animated!) to render on your current conditions screen. These aren't going to be phenomenal works of art, unless you choose to modify them to be a lot nicer than mine.

If you're keeping your work in version control, you might want to make a separate branch for this chapter. If not, copy the entire project to a separate directory so you have a backup.

This chapter is a huge amount of fun (at least, it was fun to write!), but you'll be reverting a lot of these explorations at the end of it. It'll be easier if you make a copy now.

A Conditions Widget

Start by adding an UnknownConditions widget to the KV file using a dynamic class, as shown in Example 5-1.

Example 5-1. A simple conditions widget

```
<UnknownConditions@BoxLayout>:
    conditions: ""
    canvas:
        Color:
            rgb: [0.2, 0.2, 0.2]
        Ellipse:
            pos: self.pos
            size: self.size
    Label:
        text: root.conditions
```

There are a few things to notice about this short snippet. The first is that there is a Label widget, just like you've seen in previous examples. I point this out because it is not immediately obvious that you can simultaneously have graphics instructions and child widgets. It is probably more common to do this with layouts that give more control over widget position than BoxLayout. For example, you might use a widget as a positioned sprite that moves in front of a background for a mobile game.

Second, notice the canvas property. If you want to interact with graphics primitives, you need to create instructions on a canvas. Here, you construct two instruction objects, a Color instruction and an Ellipse instruction. These have attributes such as the RGB (red green blue) Color value and the size and position of the Ellipse.

Unlike normal widgets, which are considered independent objects rendered on the screen, instructions should be thought of in aggregate. They can affect each other sequentially. Thus, the Color instruction, which says "do things in gray," affects the next instruction, which says "draw an ellipse." Together, they say "draw a gray ellipse."

Thus, even though a similar syntax is used to lay out objects and properties on a widget, it is better to think of instructions as verbs—that is, actions—while widgets are better thought of as nouns.

Finally, observe how the Ellipse instruction is able to reference properties on the self object. In a canvas, self refers to the object on which the canvas is being rendered. Thus, canvas is a property of self, not a new child widget. The ellipse is being drawn to take up the entire area of the self object, with the same position and size as the parent widget.

Now render this conditions object in the CurrentWeather KV definition by replacing the Label that currently renders conditions as a string with Example 5-2. (I don't know what "proximity shower rain" means, even if I look out my Palo Alto window.)

Example 5-2. Rendering the conditions widget

```
BoxLayout:
    id: conditions
    UnknownConditions:
        conditions: root.conditions
```

The encompassing BoxLayout is given an id so that later you can easily change the child widget to something different depending on the current weather conditions.

If you render the weather now, it will look like Figure 5-1.

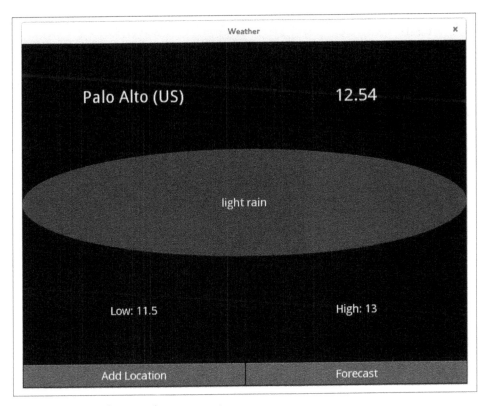

Figure 5-1. Your first graphics instruction

Dynamic Conditions

While it might be reasonable to render unknown weather as a gray ellipse, you really want things to be more dynamic. One option is to make the conditions property into a widget instead of a string and then render whatever the chosen widget is from the Python code.

See if you can work out how to do this as an exercise; you've done something just like it in a previous chapter. Create a new method called render_conditions on the Cur rentWeather class that uses Factory to construct an UnknownConditions object. If you have trouble, refer to the KV file in Example 5-3 and the Python code in Example 5-4.

Example 5-3. Referring to widget by id

```
<CurrentWeather>:
    orientation: "vertical"
    conditions: conditions       ❶
    BoxLayout:
        Label:
            text: "{} ({})".format(root.location[0], root.location[1])
```

```
        font_size: "30dp"
    Label:
        text: "{}".format(root.temp)
        font_size: "30dp"
BoxLayout:
    id: conditions    ❷
```

❷   The id is still specified here, but you are no longer constructing a default Un
knownConditions.

❶   Set the value of the property to the widget with the id so it can be referenced in
Python code.

Example 5-4. Setting a widget dynamically

```
class CurrentWeather(BoxLayout):
    location = ListProperty(['New York', 'US'])
    conditions = ObjectProperty()    ❶
    temp = NumericProperty()
    temp_min = NumericProperty()
    temp_max = NumericProperty()

    def update_weather(self):
        weather_template = "http://api.openweathermap.org/data/2.5/" +
            "weather?q={},{}&units=metric"
        weather_url = weather_template.format(*self.location)
        request = UrlRequest(weather_url, self.weather_retrieved)

    def weather_retrieved(self, request, data):
        data = json.loads(data.decode()) if not isinstance(data, dict) else data
        self.render_conditions(data['weather'][0]['description'])    ❷
        self.temp = data['main']['temp']
        self.temp_min = data['main']['temp_min']
        self.temp_max = data['main']['temp_max']

    def render_conditions(self, conditions_description):
        conditions_widget = Factory.UnknownConditions()    ❸
        conditions_widget.conditions = conditions_description
        self.conditions.clear_widgets()
        self.conditions.add_widget(conditions_widget)    ❹
```

❶   Change conditions to be an ObjectProperty rather than a StringProperty.

❷   Call the new render_conditions function with the conditions string, rather
than setting the value of the string.

❸   Remember to add from kivy.factory import Factory at the top of the file.

❹   Add the widget dynamically using Python instead of having it hardcoded in the
KV file.

With this refactor, the program will still look like Figure 5-1, but now you can easily create a new widget for clear skies, as shown in Example 5-5.

Example 5-5. Drawing a little sunshine

```
<ClearConditions@BoxLayout>:
    conditions: ""
    canvas:
        Color:
            rgb: [0.8, 0.7, 0.3]
        Line:
            cap: "round"
            width: 3
            points:
                [self.center_x - (self.height / 2),
                self.center_y,
                self.center_x + (self.height / 2),
                self.center_y]
        Line:
            cap: "round"
            width: 3
            points:
                [self.center_x,
                self.center_y - (self.height / 2),
                self.center_x,
                self.center_y + (self.height / 2)]
        Line:
            cap: "round"
            width: 3
            points:
                [self.center_x - (self.height * .35355),
                self.center_y - (self.height * .35355),
                self.center_x + (self.height * .35355),
                self.center_y + (self.height * .35355)]
        Line:
            cap: "round"
            width: 3
            points:
                [self.center_x - (self.height * .35355),
                self.center_y + (self.height * .35355),
                self.center_x + (self.height * .35355),
                self.center_y - (self.height * .35355)]
        Color:
            rgb: [0.6, 0.5, 0.0]
        Ellipse:
            pos: self.center_x - ((self.height - 40) / 2), self.pos[1] + 20
            size: [self.height - 40, self.height - 40]

    Label:
        text: root.conditions
```

It'll be easier to understand the math if you first look at the effect in Figure 5-2 (your app won't look like this until you hook up the *main.py* code in a couple minutes).

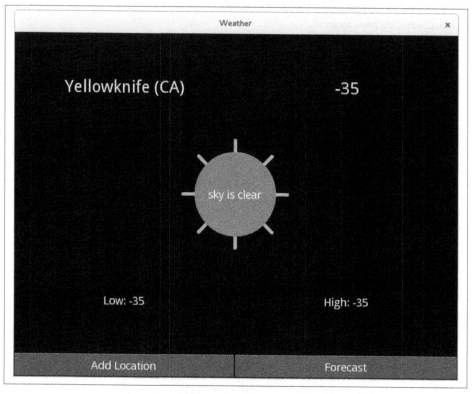

Figure 5-2. Rendering of clear, cold skies

This simple sunshine graphic is composed of some relatively simple instructions and some not completely simple mathematics. I'll describe each instruction in turn.

First, a Color instruction sets a nice yellow-orange color in RGB format. It has 80% red, 70% green, and 30% blue, since Kivy RGB settings range from 0 to 1 in floating point.

This is followed by four Line instructions. These all have the same structure, composed of cap, width, and points properties. The width is obviously the width of the line. The cap can be set to a few different values; "round" gives the ends of the line a nice radiused feeling. The points property is a list of values for the line. Alternating values are x and y coordinates in the coordinate space of the window. This means that 0, 0 is the lower-left corner of the window. Therefore, it is typically wise to adjust the points relative to the pos or center of the widget holding the canvas to which you are issuing instructions.

Each line has four values in the `points` list. These values are used to draw a single line between two points. Each of the lines is the length of the height of the widget, and is centered on the widget. The first line has the same y coordinate (the middle of the window) for both points, so it represents a horizontal line. The second similarly represents a vertical line.

The latter two lines represent a cross at a 45-degree angle to the other lines. You can safely think of the value `0.35355` as "magic" unless you know basic trigonometry, in which case it is an approximation of $\sqrt{2} / 4$, which combines the sine of 45° with a division by 2 on the height.

Finally, the color is made a bit darker, just for fun, and an ellipse with equal height and width (a circle) is drawn in front of the lines. This circle is smaller than the length of the lines, so they poke out behind it like a radix. Note my minor attempt at style: by making the color quite dark, I've made the white label readable in front of it.

Admittedly, that was not a lot of fun. It took me several minutes of fiddling to get the image to look the way I wanted it to. It isn't normal to tweak graphics primitives by hand in the KV language, though it can be useful. Mathematically derived graphics are more often created in Python code, while artistic effects should be applied as textures to an image rather than being encoded in primitives.

If you've created this widget in *weather.kv*, you might be wondering how to turn it on in *main.py*. You can do this with a simple conditional in the `render_conditions` function, as you can see in Example 5-6.

Example 5-6. Rendering different widgets depending on conditions

```
def render_conditions(self, conditions_description):
    if "clear" in conditions_description.lower():
        conditions_widget = Factory.ClearConditions()
    else:
        conditions_widget = Factory.UnknownConditions()
    conditions_widget.conditions = conditions_description
    self.conditions.clear_widgets()
    self.conditions.add_widget(conditions_widget)
```

Abstracting Common Widgets

I've mentioned in previous chapters how much you should hate duplicate code. Hopefully you were annoyed at the way the conditions label had to be applied in both `Clear Conditions` and `UnknownConditions`. Inheritance can help abstract away this duplicate code.

Note that sometimes such a refactor is not a good idea. This label adds only three lines of code per widget, and right now there are only two widgets. In this case, I probably wouldn't normally go to the trouble of refactoring, since I'd actually be adding more lines of code to maintain, and a heavy layer of abstraction.

However, as more conditions widgets are added, the duplicate code will expand. What if you later want to change the label to have a different font? Changing it in a dozen widgets would be rather irritating. Further, I want to explain this for pedagogical reasons; your own widget hierarchies are sure to be more complex than a single label.

Start by making a new class in *main.py* that extends BoxLayout. Don't forget to explicitly create the conditions property that was created dynamically in the KV classes. This property is now maintained in only one place (this class), rather than separately in the two widgets. See Example 5-7.

Example 5-7. A simple conditions widget

```
class Conditions(BoxLayout):
    conditions = StringProperty()
```

The styling for this widget in the KV language file can have the Label that was previously included in both the conditions widgets. The rule is described in Example 5-8.

Example 5-8. Basic conditions styling

```
<Conditions>:
    Label:
        text: root.conditions
```

You'll also need to modify both the widgets as described in Example 5-9. Remember to do the same thing in the more complicated ClearConditions class.

Example 5-9. The simplified UnknownConditions dynamic class

```
<UnknownConditions@Conditions>:    ❶
    canvas.before:    ❷
        Color:
            rgb: [0.2, 0.2, 0.2]
        Ellipse:
            pos: self.pos
            size: self.size
        ❸
```

❶ Extend Conditions instead of BoxLayout.

❷ Change canvas to canvas.before.

❸ Remove the conditions property and the old Label.

If you did not change canvas to canvas.before, your label would not be visible. It would render when the parent class was painted, but then the canvas would paint its graphics on top of the label. The canvas.before property is a (kind of hackish, in my opinion) way to tell Kivy to draw graphics instructions before rendering widgets. There is a similar `canvas.after` property if you want to delay rendering until later in the pipeline. After this refactor, your code will run exactly the same as previously, but now it's much more readable.

Basic Animation

Animation in Kivy can be trivially easy. I'll illustrate this with a snow widget. I'll define this widget entirely in Python rather than trying to build it in the KV language, since defining individual flakes in KV would be troublesome.

So as not to bore you, I'm not going to show you the entire process of experimentation I went through to come up with this example. However, I don't want you to get the impression that I just rattled this off the first time. Programming, especially programming involving visual design, requires a lot of trial and error. This example took about an hour to compose. I actually had a more complicated animation going, but I simplified it so the example didn't take too many pages. You can, of course, tweak it as much as you like if animation interests you.

You'll need to import a few modules that I'll explain in a moment. Add the imports from Example 5-10 to the top of your *main.py* file.

Example 5-10. Imports for snow animation

```
import random
from kivy.graphics import Color, Ellipse
from kivy.clock import Clock
```

You may as well also update `render_conditions` to render the to-be-defined widget if the conditions warrant it. See Example 5-11.

Example 5-11. Rendering the snow widget for snowy weather

```
        elif "snow" in conditions_description.lower():
            conditions_widget = SnowConditions()
```

And now, my entire animated `SnowConditions` class is displayed in Example 5-12.

Example 5-12. The animated SnowConditions class

```
class SnowConditions(Conditions):
    FLAKE_SIZE = 5      ❶
    NUM_FLAKES = 60
    FLAKE_AREA = FLAKE_SIZE * NUM_FLAKES
    FLAKE_INTERVAL = 1.0 / 30.0

    def __init__(self, **kwargs):
        super(SnowConditions, self).__init__(**kwargs)
        self.flakes = [[x * self.FLAKE_SIZE, 0]
            for x in range(self.NUM_FLAKES)]      ❷
```

```
        Clock.schedule_interval(self.update_flakes, self.FLAKE_INTERVAL)   ❸

    def update_flakes(self, time):
        for f in self.flakes:      ❹
            f[0] += random.choice([-1, 1])
            f[1] -= random.randint(0, self.FLAKE_SIZE)
            if f[1] <= 0:
                f[1] = random.randint(0, int(self.height))

        self.canvas.before.clear()
        with self.canvas.before:     ❺
            widget_x = self.center_x - self. FLAKE_AREA / 2   ❻
            widget_y = self.pos[1]
            for x_flake, y_flake in self.flakes:
                x = widget_x + x_flake     ❼
                y = widget_y + y_flake
                Color(0.9, 0.9, 1.0)     ❽
                Ellipse(pos=(x, y), size=(self.FLAKE_SIZE, self.FLAKE_SIZE))
```

❶   I defined some constants on the class to make it a little clearer what is happening
     in later code. These are pretty easy to understand from their names, except
     possibly FLAKE_INTERVAL, which says that snowflake positions will update about
     30 times per second.

❷   This list comprehension may seem rather odd. It creates a list of 60 tuples of (x,
     y) coordinates representing the position of each flake. This position is relative
     to a sort of internal reference system with (0, 0) at the bottom of a rectangular
     area that is self.height units high and FLAKE_AREA units wide. This square will
     be positioned in the center of the widget, but these (x, y) coordinates don't
     know that yet. Each flake starts equally spaced 5 units apart in the x axis at
     position 0 (the bottom) in the y axis. Why the bottom? I'll explain in a second.

❸   The Clock object is a very useful tool for animations. This call tells Kivy to call
     self.update_flakes 30 times per second.

❹   This loop does the complete job of animation. It loops over every flake's position
     and alters its coordinates. It moves each flake 1 unit either to the left or to the
     right to give it a bit of a "drifty" effect. It also moves each flake a random number
     of units down, causing the occasional "hang" effect. Finally, if the flake is at the
     bottom of the box, it is randomly popped up at some other position inside the
     box. This also repositions all the flakes after they've started at position 0.

❺   In Python, canvas instructions can be wrapped in a context manager for easier
     readability. In this case, I used canvas.before so the conditions Label in the
     parent class is still visible.

❻	The position of each flake is adjusted to be relative to the position of the widget. These coordinates represent the position in the window where the (0, 0) of the individual flakes should be positioned: centered on the widget.

❼	Add the flake position relative to the coordinate system relative to the window to get the absolute position of the flake.

❽	Graphics instructions are constructed as objects, similar to in the KV language but with more verbosity.

The picture obviously isn't animated, but my screen looks something like Figure 5-3. One of the hardest things to do in this chapter was find cities that had the weather conditions I wanted to test graphics for!

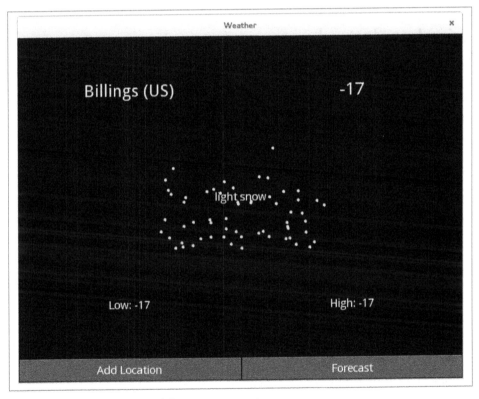

Figure 5-3. Still screenshot of the snow animation

---

super in Python 2 and Python 3

The `super` keyword has been revamped in Python 3 so that the default case is easier to write. The default case is to call "the parent class of the object that is being instantiated," and we can invoke it by passing no arguments into the `super` method.

In Python 2, you have to explicitly pass two arguments into `super:`, the current class and the `self` object. Thus, the `super` call in Example 5-12 would have to read `super(Snow Conditions, self).__init__(**kwargs)` in Python 2.

Luckily, the Python 2 syntax is still supported in Python 3, so if you are looking to support both languages, you can use the more verbose syntax and it will run on either interpreter.

Using Icons Instead

While it's fun to draw primitive graphics, doing so for all the possible weather conditions would soon become monotonous. To be honest, if I hadn't wanted to introduce you to the Kivy canvas, I would never have gone down this route at all. Instead, I would have used the weather icons supplied by Open Weather Map.

In fact, that's what I'll be doing in future chapters. You're free to keep the graphics code if you prefer, but if you want to follow along closely, you might want to revert to the state of things before you started this chapter.

Now prepare to be shocked at how easy it is to load an icon from the Internet in Kivy. See the changes to `CurrentWeather` in Example 5-13 and `weather_retrieved` in Example 5-14. Also remember to add a `conditions_image StringProperty` to the class.

Example 5-13. Using AsyncImage to load an image from the network

```
BoxLayout:
    orientation: "horizontal"
    Label:
        text: root.conditions
    AsyncImage:
        source: root.conditions_image
```

Example 5-14. Setting the conditions icon

```
self.conditions_image = "http://openweathermap.org/img/w/{}.png".format(
    data['weather'][0]['icon'])
```

The `AsyncImage` widget is an example of Kivy's modern approach to things. While most GUI toolkits would force you to download and render the image in separate steps, Kivy is aware that most applications are connected to the Web and gives us a convenient widget to grab icons from the network.

If you run this and search for Seattle, you'll almost certainly get the "light rain" icon (see Figure 5-4). It's always rainy in Seattle (this is not technically true; Seattle residents perpetuate this myth to keep the beautiful days to themselves). You don't need to write an app to know that.

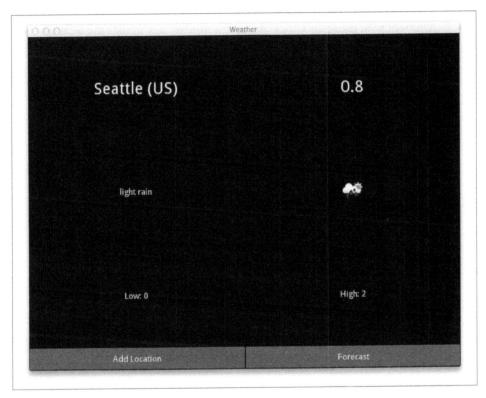

Figure 5-4. Rainy in Seattle

File It All Away

I apologize for the anticlimax of going from coding your own animation to using a stock icon. However, you're now in good shape to think about persistent storage in the next chapter! Here are a few additional paths you may want to explore:

- Add an animated rain widget inspired by the snow widget. I'd use short lines instead of circles for drops, but you could also do ellipses with little triangle hats.
- Make the snow movement more realistic. An algorithm that is a bit less random about when to hesitate or drift in a specific direction would be suitable.
- You can also experiment with randomly sized snowflakes. I did this and it looked pretty neat.

- Experiment with some of the other instructions in the Kivy API. These include Bézier curves, triangles, and meshes, as well as transform instructions such as scale and rotate.

- Read up on using textures and shaders in Kivy if you're looking to do more advanced graphics in animated games.

- Experiment with using the Clock object to automatically update the weather every hour.

## CHAPTER 6

Kivy Storage

So far, every time you run your weather app, it asks you to search for a location. It would be much more convenient if it could store your last location and render it by default.

Kivy is a Python library, which means you have access to the full gamut of Python storage modules. You could use basic file I/O, compression, encryption, pickling, JSON, SQLite3, an external SQL or NoSQL database, or any number of online storage services.

Depending on the data being stored, these are certainly useful tools worth checking out. However, Kivy also provides a simple but powerful key/value storage API for storing local data. Its primary advantage is that because Kivy is aware of the module, it works across the wide variety of platforms that Kivy uses without having to take into account filesystem structure or other differences between various operating systems.

Maintaining a List of Locations

Before looking at storing the locations, update the app to have a Locations tab. This involves nothing you haven't studied before, so you may want to think of it as an exercise. I'll try to keep this section brief so as not to bore you with knowledge you already have. If you want to skip this section, you can download the example code from O'Reilly (*http://oreil.ly/apps-kivy*) and proceed to the next section.

Here's what you need to do, step by step. As mentioned, there is some example code for the more complicated steps. Note in advance that the `ListView` of locations behaves exactly like the `ListView` for search results, so you get to reuse a lot of functionality.

1. Add a new `locations` `ObjectProperty` on `WeatherRoot` for the new `Locations` widget.
2. Turn the `args_converter` into a module-level function instead of a method, and call it as `main.locations_args_converter` in the KV file for both `ListViews`.

3. Add the new `Locations` dynamic class in KV to actually render the list of locations in a `ListView`. See Example 6-1.

4. Add a Locations button to the `CurrentWeather` widget that calls a new `show_loca tions` method on `WeatherRoot` when pressed. As Example 6-2 shows, this method is very simple.

5. Update `show_current_weather` to additionally append a new `LocationButton` to the locations `ListView`. The new code is highlighted in Example 6-3.

Example 6-1. Locations class to store the list of locations you have searched for

```
<Locations@BoxLayout>:
    orientation: "vertical"
    locations_list: locations_list    ❶
    ListView:
        id: locations_list
        adapter:
            ListAdapter(
            data=[],
            cls=main.LocationButton,
            args_converter=main.locations_args_converter)    ❷
    BoxLayout:
        orientation: "horizontal"
        size_hint_y: None
        height: "40dp"
        Button:    ❸
            text: "Add Location"
            on_press: app.root.show_add_location_form()
```

❶　　This is a dynamic class, so the `ObjectProperty` is created dynamically.

❷　　Remember to also change this function call to a module-level function in `Ad dLocationForm`, where the same `args_converter` is used.

❸　　This `Button` was moved from the `CurrentWeather` widget, where it was replaced with a `Button` to render the `Locations` view.

Example 6-2. The simple show_locations method on WeatherRoot

```
def show_locations(self):
    self.clear_widgets()
    self.add_widget(self.locations)
```

Example 6-3. The new show_current_weather function

```
def show_current_weather(self, location=None):
    self.clear_widgets()

    if self.current_weather is None:
        self.current_weather = CurrentWeather()
    if self.locations is None:    ❶
```

```
    self.locations = Factory.Locations()

if location is not None:
    self.current_weather.location = location
    if location not in self.locations.locations_list.adapter.data:        ❷
        self.locations.locations_list.adapter.data.append(location)
        self.locations.locations_list._trigger_reset_populate()

self.current_weather.update_weather()
self.add_widget(self.current_weather)
```

❶   As with `CurrentWeather`, construct the widget if it doesn't exist.

❷   If a location was specified but it isn't already in the adapter, add the data. This
       works because the `args_converter` expects a (`city, country`) tuple, which was
       passed into `show_current_weather` by the `LocationButton`.

Storing the Location List

As with most of Kivy, the `Storage` API is layered, with a generic API routing to different
backend services. This is how, for example, Kivy is able to use different audio or video
devices seamlessly, without any guidance from you.

However, with storage, you have to choose what kind of backend you will use. Kivy
currently supports three options:

- A `DictStore` that stores data in a Python dictionary in memory. This does not
  persist if the application closes.
- A `JsonStore` that stores data in JSON format on the local filesystem.
- A `RedisStore` that allows you to store data locally or remotely in a Redis filesystem.

The `DictStore` isn't too useful to you, since the adapter is already storing data in memory
on your behalf. The `RedisStore` might be useful if you wanted to sync data to a central
database where you could access it from multiple devices. However, I'll demo the `Json
Store`, which is more suitable to the use case at hand.

Constructing a `JsonStore` is very easy. In this case, you should build it as an instance
property on the `WeatherRoot` class. This means you'll have to override the `__init__`
method as shown in Example 6-4, first adding an import for `from kivy.storage.json
store import JsonStore` at the top of the file.

Example 6-4. Initializer for WeatherRoot

```
def __init__(self, **kwargs):
    super(WeatherRoot, self).__init__(**kwargs)        ❶
    self.store = JsonStore("weather_store.json")
```

❶ Remember, Python 3 can use super without arguments. I can never remember which order the arguments go in, so Python 3 saves me a lot of trial and error!

Kivy permits multiple inheritance and automatic property assignment by never passing positional arguments into the __init__ method. Thus, you should accept arbitrary kwargs and pass them up to the parent class, just in case. Give the object a relative filename. The store should take care of ensuring it's saved to a reasonable location that can be found again on different devices.

Then you can use the put method to store the known locations whenever a new one is added. Do this only when a new item is appended to the ListView inside the conditionals in show_current_weather. See Example 6-5.

Example 6-5. Putting a value to the store when a location is added

```
if location not in self.locations.locations_list.adapter.data:
    self.locations.locations_list.adapter.data.append(location)
    self.locations.locations_list._trigger_reset_populate()
    self.store.put("locations",
        locations=list(self.locations.locations_list.adapter.data))
```

 Note that put requires one positional key and then an arbitrary number of named values. Each value is passed as a keyword argument. In this case, I supplied only one argument, locations, where the value is a list of tuple objects. This serializes easily to JSON inside the store. If you call put again, it will overwrite *all* the values for that key, even if you specify different values.

Finally, if the store exists, load the data into the adapter after constructing the Locations object in show_current_weather, as shown in Example 6-6.

Example 6-6. Loading data from the store

```
if self.locations is None:
    self.locations = Factory.Locations()
    if (self.store.exists('locations')):
        locations = self.store.get("locations")['locations']
        self.locations.locations_list.adapter.data.extend(locations)
```

Note that get returns a dictionary where the keys are any keyword arguments you passed into put for that key.

See if you can work out how to store the current location in the same key and, if it is set, render it when the application starts. Example 6-7 in show_current_weather and Example 6-8 in the WeatherRoot initializer demonstrate how simple this can be.

Example 6-7. Putting the current location

```
if location is not None:
    self.current_weather.location = location
    if location not in self.locations.locations_list.adapter.data:
        self.locations.locations_list.adapter.data.append(location)
        self.locations.locations_list._trigger_reset_populate()
        self.store.put("locations",
            locations=list(self.locations.locations_list.adapter.data),
            current_location=location)
```

Example 6-8. Loading the current location and rendering

```
def __init__(self, **kwargs):
    super(WeatherRoot, self).__init__(**kwargs)
    self.store = JsonStore("weather_store.json")
    if self.store.exists('locations'):
        current_location = self.store.get("locations")["current_location"]
        self.show_current_weather(current_location)
```

The User Settings Dialog

Kivy has built-in support for storing user settings backed by a configuration file. In fact, Kivy has a bunch of built-in configuration settings that the user can change. You don't have to do anything to enable these; they're already there. On your desktop machine, just press F1 to display the settings, as shown in Figure 6-1.

 The default settings are pretty technical and a bit overwhelming for the average user. Depending on your use case, you might want to leave them in, as I did in this chapter for pedagogical reasons. However, if you want to hide them, it's as simple as adding a use_kivy_set tings = False line to the WeatherApp class.

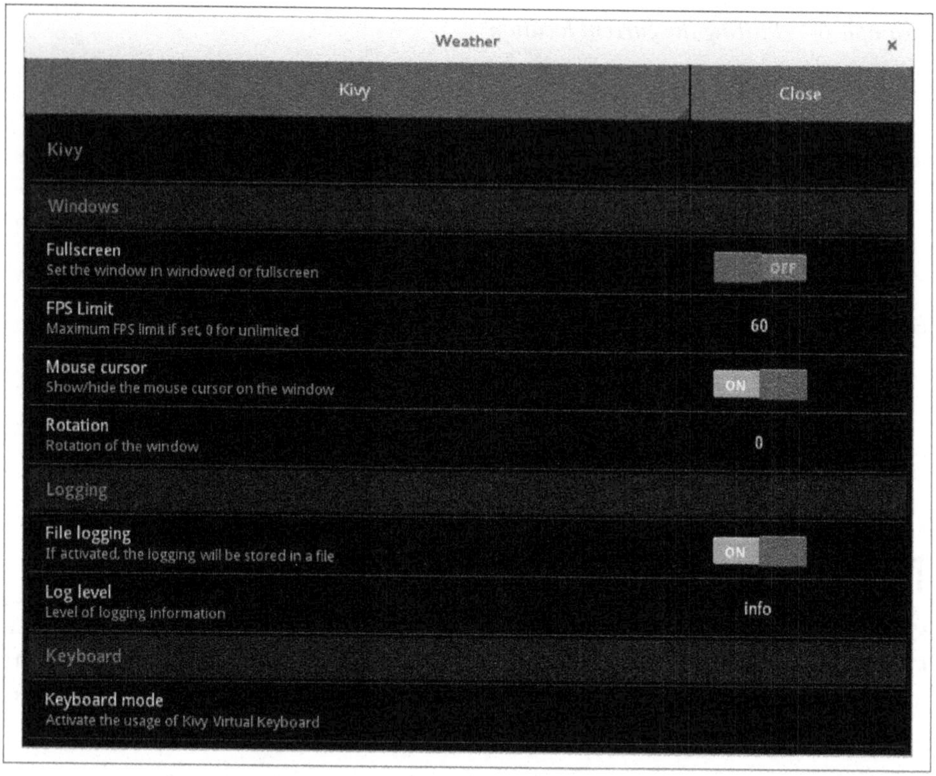

Figure 6-1. Kivy settings dialog

The Kivy settings are stored in a user-editable *.ini* file named after your application class, with the same name mangling used to guess the *.kv* filename. Thus, the settings for the WeatherApp class appear in *weather.ini*.

Don't ship this file with your application. Instead, add a build_config method to your WeatherApp class. It will automatically generate the file the first time it is called. This method should set up the structure of the file and all default values for your app. Remember, an *.ini* file has sections with key/value pairs inside each section. For this example, I'll just add one configuration setting: what system to render the temperatures in. Put it in the General section, as shown in build_config in Example 6-9.

The next step is to configure your settings panel to allow the user to change these settings. We must do this using JSON, for reasons I don't understand (I would have used a KV language syntax).

The build_settings method in Example 6-9 demonstrates how to do this.

Example 6-9. Creating a settings panel and configuration management

```
class WeatherApp(App):
    def build_config(self, config):
        config.setdefaults('General', {'temp_type': "Metric"})

    def build_settings(self, settings):
        settings.add_json_panel("Weather Settings", self.config, data="""
            [
                {"type": "options",
                    "title": "Temperature System",
                    "section": "General",
                    "key": "temp_type",
                    "options": ["Metric", "Imperial"]
                }
            ]"""
        )
```

The key invocation here is the `add_json_panel` call, which accepts three arguments. The first is the title of the panel, as rendered in the settings dialog. It's possible to have multiple settings panels, including the default Kivy panel you saw earlier. The second parameter is almost always `self.config`, the configuration object that was set up in `build_config`. Finally, you can supply either `filename` or `data` as a keyword argument to load JSON data from a file or string.

The example uses the `data` argument and encodes the data inline. The options are straightforward, but fairly verbose considering that I am describing only one setting object.

The `type` defines how the setting is rendered. I chose `options` since I want to select between two choices. Other values `type` can take include:

- `bool`
- `numeric`
- `string`
- `path`
- `title` (acts as a placeholder between sections)

The `title` is the user-readable label to give the setting inside the dialog. The `section` parameter maps directly to whatever section you specified in `config.setdefaults`, while key maps to a key inside the dictionary passed into that function. Finally, since this is an `options` setting, the actual options are specified in a JSON list.

If you run the program and press F1, you're given a very simple settings panel, as shown in Figure 6-2.

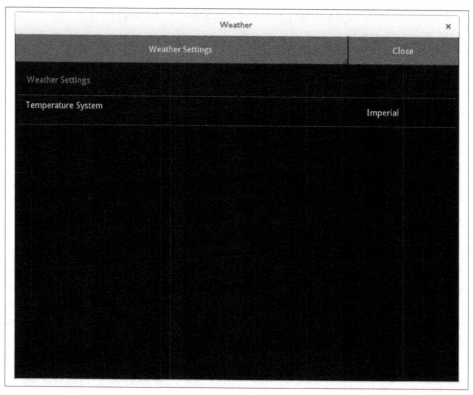

Figure 6-2. Temperature system setting

The setting is saved by default as soon as the user closes the dialog. The next time the program runs, the user's choice is rendered instead of the default.

The next step, of course, is to actually use this setting in production. This requires some minor changes to update_weather so that you are requesting the appropriate units from Open Weather Map. See Example 6-10.

Example 6-10. Requesting data in the user's selected measuring system

```
def update_weather(self):
    config = WeatherApp.get_running_app().config       ❶
    temp_type = config.getdefault("General", "temp_type", "metric").lower()   ❷
    weather_template = "http://api.openweathermap.org/data/2.5/" +
        "weather?q={},{}&units={}"   ❸
    weather_url = weather_template.format(
        self.location[0],
        self.location[1],
        temp_type)   ❹
    request = UrlRequest(weather_url, self.weather_retrieved)
```

❶ get_running_app is a static method that returns the singleton running app. Simply request the config variable from it.

❷ getdefault returns the value stored in the configuration in the temp_type key under the General section. If that section or key doesn't exist, it returns the default value, metric.

❸ weather_template is changed to have the units passed in a format string instead of being hardcoded (removing hardcoded values should yield a tremendous sense of accomplishment).

❹ The template string now needs to have three values substituted in the format call.

This should now be working fine, with one small bug. If you press F1 from the CurrentLocation view, it doesn't update the display until update_weather is called, which requires you to select a different location.

Luckily, you can listen for changes by adding an on_config_change method to the WeatherApp class. This method calls update_weather immediately, as shown in Example 6-11. This example uses the "ask forgiveness rather than permission" approach to determine if the current root window has an update_weather function. I suspect this will be useful when we implement the Forecast tab in the next chapter.

Example 6-11. Updating weather on_config_change

```
def on_config_change(self, config, section, key, value):
    if config is self.config and key == "temp_type":
        try:
            self.root.children[0].update_weather()
        except AttributeError:
            pass
```

Last, add a button to display the settings window manually. Users don't necessarily know that the F1 key will display the settings window. Kivy will map the menu button on Android devices to the settings window, but modern Android devices don't have a menu key.

For brevity, I'm just going to throw a button on the Locations window to display settings. This isn't exactly good interface design, but Example 6-12 will get the pertinent points across.

Example 6-12. A button to display the settings

```
Button:
    text: "Settings"
    on_press: app.open_settings()
```

File It All Away

I have to tell you, folks, I'm surprised at how easy this chapter was to write. I haven't used the settings or storage APIs before. I knew from my experience with other Kivy APIs that it would be simple, but I was able to write, test, and document all these examples in a single day! I hope this chapter was as informative and fun for you as it was for me.

There are, as always, numerous activities you can try to extend your knowledge on your own. Try some of these, for example:

- The code that updates the results list after the user searches for a location is very similar to the code that updates the list of locations when one is selected. I think this could be elegantly refactored into a single `LocationListView` class that has methods that take care of updating the data and calling the `trigger_reset_popu late` function.

- The `Locations` view has no way to remove a location once it's added. Explore ways to solve this. Personally, I'd look at extending `LocationButton` to have a button inside it (yes, it is possible to have a button on a button) that connects to a `re move` token. Remember to update the `JsonStore` object, too.

- I think it would be elegant if there were a version of `ListAdapter` that automatically stored its value inside a `JsonStore` object whenever it was updated. I wouldn't be surprised if the Kivy team would accept a pull request with such an adapter if you were up for some open source contribution!

- Add some more settings for fun. One thing you might try is conditionally rendering additional data (such as humidity or wind speed) depending on whether the user has requested it. Or you could set an option for how often the weather should be updated using the `Clock` object, if you did the last exercise in the previous chapter.

## CHAPTER 7

Gestures

Kivy was designed from the ground up with fingers, rather than pointing devices, in mind as a primary method of input. You haven't had much direct interaction with input devices in this book; instead, we've focused on touch events that are built into widgets supplied with Kivy. Buttons can be pressed, inputs can have text entered into them, and ListViews can be scrolled with a gesture.

In this chapter, you'll delve a bit deeper into Kivy's event system and add a few basic gestures to the app. The gestures will be *swipe left* and *swipe right* on the current weather and forecast widgets, which will switch to the other widget. The *swipe down* gesture will be used to refresh the weather. This is a fairly standard interaction feature in mobile computing.

The Forecast Tab

First, take some time to implement the forecast widget, so you have something to use gestures to switch between. As in Chapter 6, this should be old hat for you, so I'm just going to summarize the changes. Then I can focus on giving you new and interesting content! I recommend you try to implement these steps before referring to the example code.

1. Create a mockup of how you would like the forecast to look. Bear in mind that your widget has to fit on a narrow mobile screen. See Figure 7-1.

2. Add a ForecastLabel class to *weather.kv* to render individual forecast data. Put an icon, conditions, and temperature min and max on it. See Example 7-1.

3. Add a Forecast class extending BoxLayout to *main.py* and *weather.kv*. Give it a BoxLayout with a named id so that ForecastLabel objects can be added to it later. Also give it a button to switch to the CurrentWeather widget and hook up the event listener. See Example 7-1.

4. Create an `update_weather` method on `Forecast` that downloads three days' worth of weather (remember to query the config for metrics) from Open Weather Map's forecast page and creates three `ForecastLabel` objects on the BoxLayout. You'll probably want to import and use Python's datetime module here (see Example 7-2).

5. Create an appropriate `show_forecast` function on `WeatherRoot`, as shown in Example 7-3. Also hook up event listeners to call it from the button on `Current Weather`.

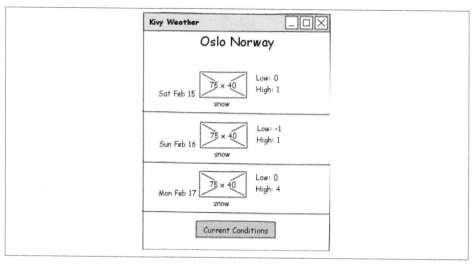

Figure 7-1. A three-day forecast

Example 7-1. ForecastLabel and Forecast classes

```
<ForecastLabel@BoxLayout>:
    date: ""
    conditions_image: ""
    conditions: ""
    temp_min: None
    temp_max: None
    canvas.before:
        Color:
            rgb: [0.2, 0.2, 0.2]
        Line:
            points: [self.pos[0], self.pos[1], self.width, self.pos[1]]
    Label:
        text: root.date
    BoxLayout:
        orientation: "vertical"
        AsyncImage:
            source: root.conditions_image
        Label:
```

```
            text: root.conditions
    BoxLayout:
        orientation: "vertical"
        Label:
            text: "Low: {}".format(root.temp_min)
        Label:
            text: "High: {}".format(root.temp_max)

<Forecast>:
    forecast_container: forecast_container
    orientation: "vertical"
    Label:
        size_hint_y: 0.1
        font_size: "30dp"
        text: "{} ({})".format(root.location[0], root.location[1])
    BoxLayout:
        orientation: "vertical"
        id: forecast_container
    BoxLayout:
        orientation: "horizontal"
        size_hint_y: None
        height: "40dp"
        Button:
            text: "Current"
            on_press: app.root.show_current_weather(root.location)
```

Example 7-2. Forecast class with update_weather method

```python
class Forecast(BoxLayout):
    location = ListProperty(['New York', 'US'])
    forecast_container = ObjectProperty()

    def update_weather(self):
        config = WeatherApp.get_running_app().config
        temp_type = config.getdefault("General", "temp_type", "metric").lower()
        weather_template = "http://api.openweathermap.org/data/2.5/forecast/" + \
            "daily?q={},{}&units={}&cnt=3"
        weather_url = weather_template.format(
            self.location[0],
            self.location[1],
            temp_type)
        request = UrlRequest(weather_url, self.weather_retrieved)

    def weather_retrieved(self, request, data):
        data = json.loads(data.decode()) if not isinstance(data, dict) else data
        self.forecast_container.clear_widgets()
        for day in data['list']:
            label = Factory.ForecastLabel()
            label.date = datetime.datetime.fromtimestamp(day['dt']).strftime(
                "%a %b %d")

            label.conditions = day['weather'][0]['description']
            label.conditions_image = "http://openweathermap.org/img/w/{}.png".format(
```

```
            day['weather'][0]['icon'])
        label.temp_min = day['temp']['min']
        label.temp_max = day['temp']['max']
        self.forecast_container.add_widget(label)
```

Example 7-3. show_forecast method

```
def show_forecast(self, location=None):
    self.clear_widgets()

    if self.forecast is None:
        self.forecast = Factory.Forecast()

    if location is not None:
        self.forecast.location = location

    self.forecast.update_weather()
    self.add_widget(self.forecast)
```

As Figure 7-2 shows, the forecast widget isn't beautiful, but it gets the job done.

Figure 7-2. Seattle is going to get snow

Recording Gestures

The mathematics behind computational gesture recognition are quite complicated. Luckily, the Kivy developers have supplied a basic gesture library that allows you to record a gesture using an example tool, and then match user input gestures against the recording to test if it's the same gesture. Sound simple? It's not hard, but the process is a bit involved.

The first thing you want to do is to record the encoded representation of the three gestures you want to recognize. Do this using the *gesture_board.py* example that ships with Kivy. Hopefully you already have the Kivy source code checked out, either because you built it from scratch in Chapter 1 or because you've been diligently reading through the source when you get stuck trying to understand something and the documentation is insufficient. If not, check it out with the command `git clone http://github.com/kivy/kivy`.

Getting Git

If you use Linux, Git is probably preinstalled, since Linux is a developer's operating system. Git was originally designed for the distributed development of the Linux kernel and is an integral part of modern Linux development culture. If it's not installed, it'll be a simple process to install it using your distribution's package manager.

If you've configured Mac OS for development by installing Apple's XCode, you will also have Git installed. You're going to need to do this anyway if you want to deploy to iOS devices, and XCode contains a dazzling number of other tools that may or may not be useful in your future endeavors as a developer on an Apple machine.

If you use Windows, you'll want to install the MSysGit package (*http://msys git.github.io*). Windows was once considered a second-class citizen for Git usage, but MSysGit changes this. In addition to giving you the Git version control tool, it also provides an easy installer for the powerful bash command-line shell. You can (and should) use this shell instead of the default Windows command prompt for all your development, not just Git.

Then, in a terminal, `cd` into the *kivy/examples/gestures* directory. Run the command `python gesture_board.py`.

This will pop up a familiar black window. It looks like the default blank Kivy window with no widgets on it. This is a bit misleading, though, because it does have a widget that is designed to recognize Kivy gestures. The demo comes with four gestures preinstalled. If you draw a clockwise circular shape on the screen, as shown in Figure 7-3, you should get some output on the terminal similar to Example 7-4.

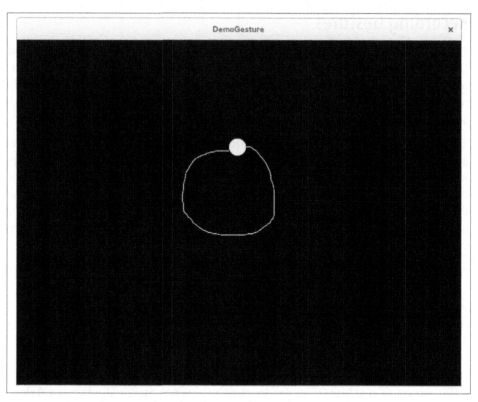

Figure 7-3. A circular gesture

Example 7-4. Output after drawing a circular gesture

```
gesture representation: <a very long random string of characters>
cross: 0.3540801575248498
check: -2.4878193071394503
circle: 0.9506637523286905
square: 0.7579676451240299
(0.9506637523286905, <kivy.gesture.Gesture object at 0x7f513df07450>)
circle
```

Read this output from bottom to top. The last line of the output indicates that the app (correctly) guessed that I drew a circle. The line above that indicates the actual gesture object that was matched and with what confidence. The four lines of text above that provide the matching scores for the four sample gestures. Unless I happened to draw exactly the same circle that whoever recorded these gestures did, I will not get a score of 1.0, but the closer it is to 1.0 the more likely it is that my drawing is a representation of the same gesture.

The first line of text, which I snipped out of this example to save you from having to read a page full of gibberish (and O'Reilly from having to print it), is a textual representation of the gesture I drew. Don't bother trying to interpret it; it's meaningless in this form. However, this line (likely several lines since it wraps across your terminal, but there's no newline character, so treat it as a single line) is the information you need to record if you want to create your own gestures and match them.

So, we'll do that next. There are three gestures you want to record: a left-to-right horizontal line, a right-to-left horizontal line, and a bottom-to-top vertical line. They are pretty simple gestures. Create a new Python file named *gesture_box.py*. Put each string inside a dictionary named `gesture_strings`, as summarized in Example 7-5, bearing in mind that your strings will be both different and longer.

Example 7-5. Summary of three gestures

```
gesture_strings = {
    'left_to_right_line': 'eNp91XtsU...<snip>...4hSE=',
    'right_to_left_line': 'eNp91UlME...<snip>...Erg==',
    'bottom_to_top_line': 'eNp91HlsD...<snip>...NMndJz'
}
```

Now you need to write some code to convert those strings back into the format that Kivy recognizes as gestures. In the same *gesture_box.py* file, add some imports and construct a `GestureDatabase`, as shown in Example 7-6.

Example 7-6. Constructing a GestureDatabase

```
from kivy.gesture import GestureDatabase

gestures = GestureDatabase()
for name, gesture_string in gesture_strings.items():
    gesture = gestures.str_to_gesture(gesture_string)
    gesture.name = name
    gestures.add_gesture(gesture)
```

Now you have a module-level database of gestures. This database can compare gestures the user makes to its three stored gestures and tell us if the user input matches any of them.

Touch Events

The next step is to record the gestures that the user makes on the screen. My plan is to create a new widget that listens to input touch events, distinguishes gestures, and fires new events for each gesture it recognizes. In short, you're about to learn a lot more about Kivy's event system!

Start by creating a new class named `GestureBox` in *gesture_box.py*. Make it extend `BoxLayout` (remember to import the `BoxLayout` class, since it isn't available in this file yet).

You've worked with higher-level events in most of the previous chapters. Now it's time to get a little closer to the hardware. Kivy is designed with touchscreens in mind, so you'll be working with touch events, even if you're using a mouse.

There are three different kinds of touch events:

- touch_down, which corresponds to the user touching a finger on the touchscreen or pressing the mouse button.
- touch_move, which corresponds to the user dragging a finger after touching it onto the screen, or dragging the mouse with the button down. There may be multiple (or no) move events between a down and an up event.
- touch_up, which corresponds to lifting the finger off the screen or releasing the mouse button.

Kivy has full multitouch support, so it's possible for more than one touch_down-initiated touch event to be active at one time. The down, move, and up events are linked for each touch, such that you can access in the touch_move and touch_up events data that was set earlier in the touch_down event. You do this by passing a touch argument into the event handlers that contains data about the touch itself, and to which you can add arbitrary data in typical Pythonic fashion.

To recognize a gesture, you'll need to start recording each individual event in the touch_down handler, add the data points for each call to touch_move, and then do the gesture calculations when all data points have been received in the touch_up handler. Refer to Example 7-7.

Example 7-7. GestureBox down, up, and move events

```
class GestureBox(BoxLayout):
    def on_touch_down(self, touch):
        touch.ud['gesture_path'] = [(touch.x, touch.y)]
        super(GestureBox, self).on_touch_down(touch)

    def on_touch_move(self, touch):
        touch.ud['gesture_path'].append((touch.x, touch.y))
        super(GestureBox, self).on_touch_move(touch)

    def on_touch_up(self, touch):
        print(touch.ud['gesture_path'])
        super(GestureBox, self).on_touch_up(touch)
```

As with other Kivy events, you can hook up event handlers in your Python code by implementing on_eventname_. The touch object passed into each event has a ud (short for user data) dictionary that is the same for each event. Construct a gesture_path list in the down event, append each subsequent motion event to it in the move event, and then simply print it in the up event. Each event also calls its super method so that the buttons at the bottom of the screen still work.

Now, to test this code, modify the *main.py* file to include a from gesture_box import GestureBox import. Then make the CurrentWeather and Forecast widgets extend this new class instead of BoxLayout. The layout functionality will be the same. However, if you now drag the mouse on these widgets, you will see a collection of points output on the terminal when you release the button.

Recognizing Gestures

Now that you have the points that the user created available, you can construct a Ges ture object. Then you simply have to invite the GestureDatabase object to detect whether or not the user's input matches any of the gestures you created. Example 7-8 demonstrates.

Example 7-8. Recognizing if a gesture occurred

```
def on_touch_up(self, touch):
    if 'gesture_path' in touch.ud:
        gesture = Gesture()  ❶
        gesture.add_stroke(touch.ud['gesture_path'])  ❷
        gesture.normalize()  ❸
        match = gestures.find(gesture, minscore=0.90)  ❹
        if match:
            print("{} happened".format(match[1].name))  ❺
    super(GestureBox, self).on_touch_up(touch)
```

❶ You'll also want a from kivy.gesture import Gesture at the top of the file.

❷ The add_stroke method accepts the list of (x, y) tuples that have been attached to the user data in the down and move methods.

❸ Normalizing a gesture basically forces it to be converted to a unit box. This means that gestures that have the same shape, but different sizes, will match at each point.

❹ minscore represents how confident the algorithm is that the gesture matches anything in the database. It will return the highest-matching gesture, provided the match is higher than this score.

❺ The match object returns a tuple of (score, gesture). The name of the gesture was stored with each gesture when the GestureDatabase was populated. Here, you just print it.

Firing Events

Of course, it isn't much use to just print that a gesture happened. It would be better to fire a new event that other classes can interpret. This is reminiscent of how you listen for press events rather than touch_down events on a button.

So, time to create a new event! Instead of creating a single on_gesture event, I'm going to dynamically create a new event type for each of the three gestures I've defined. I'll end up with on_left_to_right_line, on_right_to_left_line, and on_bottom_to_top_line events. This might not be the most sensible design, but it does make it trivial to respond to individual gestures from inside the KV language file.

The first step is to register the new event type with the EventDispatcher. Every widget extends the EventDispatcher class, so we can do this trivially inside a new __init__ method on the GestureBox class in *gesture_box.py*, as shown in Example 7-9.

You also need to add default event handlers for each of those events, also shown in Example 7-9. The default activity can be to do nothing, but the methods still need to exist.

Example 7-9. Registering new event types

```
def __init__(self, **kwargs):
    for name in gesture_strings:
        self.register_event_type('on_{}'.format(name))
    super(GestureBox, self).__init__
    (**kwargs)

def on_left_to_right_line(self):
    pass

def on_right_to_left_line(self):
    pass

def on_bottom_to_top_line(self):
    pass
```

Then all you have to do to fire an event is call the self.dispatch method, optionally passing any arguments that you would like to arrive with the event. In Example 7-10 I don't pass any arguments, since gestures are binary (either they happened or they didn't) and there is no data to supply. If you created a generic on_gesture event instead of different events for each gesture, you might pass in the gesture name as an argument. In this case, the call would be self.dispatch(on_gesture, gesture.name).

Example 7-10. Firing an event with self.dispatch

```
if match:
    self.dispatch('on_{}'.format(match[1].name))
```

Now that your events are firing reliably, you can add a few event handlers to your KV language file, as shown in Example 7-11 and Example 7-12.

Example 7-11. Handling the gesture events on CurrentWeather

```
<CurrentWeather>:
    orientation: "vertical"
    on_right_to_left_line: app.root.show_forecast(root.location)
    on_bottom_to_top_line: root.update_weather()
```

Example 7-12. Handling gesture events on the Forecast widget

```
<Forecast>:
    forecast_container: forecast_container
    orientation: "vertical"

    on_left_to_right_line: app.root.show_current_weather(root.location)
    on_bottom_to_top_line: root.update_weather()
```

File It All Away

At this point, you have a fully functional weather app with the current conditions and a three-day forecast. You can switch between the two views with a simple gesture. There are a few areas of further exploration that you can study:

- The Locations, CurrentWeather, and Forecast classes all contain a BoxLayout that has several properties (orientation, size_hint_y, and height) in common. Refactor the KV code so that these properties are stored in a dynamic class named ButtonBar.

- For practice, add a new gesture (maybe down or a curve or circle) that does something interesting. If you want to get fancy, look into multitouch gestures. There isn't a lot of documentation on this, but it is doable.

- Experiment with creating new events. Perhaps you could add something to the update_weather method to fire an event if the temperature changes.

- You can make the GestureBox initializer dynamically create the default event handlers by calling setattr on self and attaching an empty method to it. This way, you won't have to create a new default handler if you add a new gesture.

## CHAPTER 8

Advanced Widgets

Your weather app is now fully functional and you could do an initial release already. However, there are a few things you can do to make it better. This chapter is a large code refactor. The functionality won't change very much, but the usability will improve and the amount of code involved will shrink, which means fewer bugs and easier maintenance.

Kivy has an abundant collection of built-in widgets, and this book can't cover all of them. In this chapter, you'll see three of them in detail: the `Carousel`, `ModalView`, and `Action Bar`. These widgets will largely replace much of the screen management code you have written manually so far.

Be prepared. This will be a large refactor, and you will probably have to do quite a bit of debugging to get everything working correctly. This is great real-world practice, though, as reworking existing code is an important part of the software development process. Applications that don't evolve over time are inevitably superceded.

Before you start, remove your brand new *gesture_box.py* file altogether and revert the two classes in *main.py* to extend `BoxLayout` instead of `GestureBox`. You'll also need to remove an `import` statement.

Also remove the custom gesture event listeners (such as `on_right_to_left_line`) from the KV language file.

If your refactor begins with removing entire files of custom code that you no longer have to maintain, you're probably doing something right!

Carousel

The `Carousel` widget allows for swiping between multiple widgets in a screen. This is a large part of what you implemented manually in Chapter 7 (if you're wondering why

I didn't implement Carousel in the first place, it's because I wanted to give you some lower-level experience with Kivy events). However, Carousel adds fancy animation and takes care of several edge cases that I ignored while presenting that chapter.

The three widgets Carousel will switch between are Locations, CurrentWeather, and ForecastLabel. Ignore the AddLocationForm widget for now. You will now be adding all these widgets in the KV file instead of trying to create them dynamically in Python. Hook each existing ObjectProperty to a widget id, as shown in Example 8-1, and remember to add a new carousel = ObjectProperty() to the WeatherRoot widget in *main.py*.

Example 8-1. Adding a carousel to WeatherRoot

```
<WeatherRoot>:
    carousel: carousel
    locations: locations
    current_weather: current_weather
    forecast: forecast
    Carousel:
        id: carousel
        Locations:
            id: locations
        CurrentWeather:
            id: current_weather
        Forecast:
            id: forecast
```

 Crash alert: you'll probably have to delete your *weather_store.json* file before running this example successfully, and don't click the Add Location button. This will get fixed in the next section.

If you run the program now, you'll discover that all the weather functionality is broken, but you can drag the mouse left and right on the screen to easily switch between the three widgets. That's progress… right?

You'll also find that the buttons on the bottom bar only sort of work. As you'll recall, each of these manually replaces the contents of the WeatherRoot widget with a new child. This means that the Carousel is removed. Thus, after you've clicked a button, the swipe actions no longer work.

To solve this, set the button clicks to do nothing more than change slides on the Carousel. For example, in the CurrentWeather widget, the two buttons will look like Example 8-2.

Example 8-2. Event handlers on the CurrentWeather buttons

```
Button:
    text: "Locations"
    on_press: app.root.carousel.load_slide(app.root.locations)
Button:
    text: "Forecast"
    on_press: app.root.carousel.load_slide(app.root.forecast)
```

Remember to make similar changes to the button on the Forecast slide.

You'll be doing more refactoring on the code in *main.py* later, but in order to see those future changes working, fix up the AddLocationForm widget next.

The ModalView Widget

ModalView and its more featureful subclass, Popup, allow widgets to be displayed in front of existing widgets. This is what you should use for displaying the Add Location form instead of completely replacing the contents of the root widget.

This particular refactor involves just a few changes, but they're spread all over both files. First make the AddLocationForm class in *main.py* extend ModalView (which you will need to import as from kivy.uix.modalview import ModalView). Then replace the show_add_location_form method on WeatherRoot with Example 8-3, remembering to add a new add_location_form = ObjectProperty() to the WeatherRoot object.

Example 8-3. Using ModalView.open to render a view

```
def show_add_location_form(self):
    self.add_location_form = AddLocationForm()
    self.add_location_form.open()
```

If you run this code and click the Add Location button, you may be in for a bit of a surprise. As Figure 8-1 illustrates, the widgets were all drawn on top of each other instead of being laid out as expected.

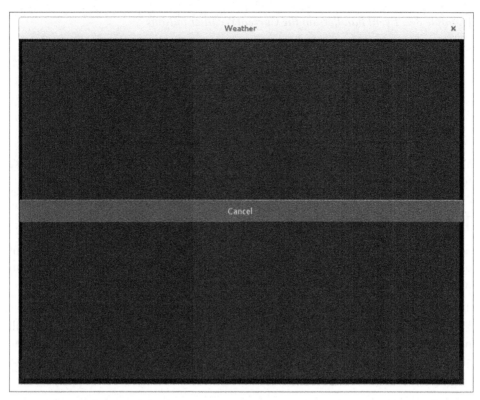

Figure 8-1. The layout of the form is completely broken

This oversight is because ModalView does not extend BoxLayout. To get the old behavior back, simply wrap the entire contents of AddLocationForm in the *weather.kv* file with an extra BoxLayout, as shown in Example 8-4.

Example 8-4. BoxLayout as the child of ModalView

```
<AddLocationForm>:
    search_input: search_box
    search_results: search_results_list
    BoxLayout:      ❶
        orientation: "vertical"     ❷
        BoxLayout:
            height: "40dp"
            size_hint_y: None
            TextInput:
                id: search_box
```

❶   The new BoxLayout now has everything below it further indented.

❷   The orientation property is moved from the parent widget to the BoxLayout.

Now the form will render as you are used to. Change the on_press event on the Cancel button to dismiss the dialog instead of calling show_current_weather. Example 8-5 illustrates.

Example 8-5. The Cancel button event handler

```
Button:
    height: "40dp"
    size_hint_y: None
    text: "Cancel"
    on_press: root.dismiss()
```

Completing the Refactor

The next step is to clean up WeatherRoot, especially the show_current_weather method. Start, however, by outright removing a couple of methods that are no longer required:

- show_locations has been superceded by the selection of a slide on the Carousel.
- show_forecast has also been superceded. The act of updating the forecast will be moved into the show_current_weather method shortly.

Next, remove the code from show_current_weather that clears the current widget as well as the two conditionals that construct CurrentWeather and Locations widgets if they don't exist. In the Carousel, these widgets always exist, even when they aren't visible.

Before removing the locations conditional, note that it contains some code for updating the locations from a store. If you were doing this refactor without my guidance, I would recommend updating your to-do list (it's a good idea to start refactors with a text file listing the things you need to complete) to include "update locations from the store" so you don't forget that functionality when the refactor is complete.

Your code is no longer calling this method with a possible location=None parameter, so you can call the location-updating code without checking the conditional.

Now you have to add a couple of lines of code to set the location on the Forecast object as well. This slide needs to be updated as soon as the location is loaded now, instead of after it is displayed.

Next, replace the add_widget call with a call to load_slide, and finally, dismiss the add_location_form if it is visible. Remember that show_current_weather can be called both from AddLocationForm and from the Locations slide, so it may or may not be set at this time.

That was a lot of description. I hope it made sense, but if not, the new, much simpler method in Example 8-6 should compare favorably to your previous version.

Example 8-6. The new show_current_weather method

```
def show_current_weather(self, location):
    if location not in self.locations.locations_list.adapter.data:
        self.locations.locations_list.adapter.data.append(location)
        self.locations.locations_list._trigger_reset_populate()
        self.store.put("locations",
            locations=list(self.locations.locations_list.adapter.data),
            current_location=location)

    self.current_weather.location = location
    self.forecast.location = location
    self.current_weather.update_weather()
    self.forecast.update_weather()

    self.carousel.load_slide(self.current_weather)
    if self.add_location_form is not None:
        self.add_location_form.dismiss()
```

Now fix up the __init__ method on WeatherRoot to set up the stored locations list as well as the current location when the widget is constructed. Additionally, if no stored location exists, automatically pop up the Add Location form on the next clock cycle. See Example 8-7.

Example 8-7. The updated on_config_change method

```
def __init__(self, **kwargs):
    super(WeatherRoot, self).__init__(**kwargs)
    self.store = JsonStore("weather_store.json")
    if self.store.exists('locations'):
        locations = self.store.get('locations')
        self.locations.locations_list.adapter.data.extend(locations['locations'])
        current_location = locations["current_location"]
        self.show_current_weather(current_location)
    else:
        Clock.schedule_once(lambda dt: self.show_add_location_form())
```

Finally, make the on_config_change method on the WeatherApp update the weather on the CurrentWeather and Forecast widgets directly, as shown in Example 8-8. Otherwise, when you change the config setting, the values won't get set.

Example 8-8. The updated __init__ method

```
def on_config_change(self, config, section, key, value):
    if config is self.config and key == "temp_type":
        try:
            self.root.current_weather.update_weather()
            self.root.forecast.update_weather()
```

```
except AttributeError:
    pass
```

This last change illustrates a danger inherent in refactoring. I didn't notice this problem when I originally wrote this chapter. Because the exception being thrown happened to be caught by the nasty code, there were no errors to indicate that the values were not being updated when the user changed the preferred measurement unit. I picked up on it when I was writing Chapter 9, and had to come back and fix it. Be wary!

Adding an Action Bar

The Kivy API comes with an `ActionBar` widget that mimics the Android action bar, making it possible to integrate a little better with the Android ecosystem. Even without our worrying about Android integration, the `ActionBar` can give a better user experience than the buttons you have at the bottom of your existing `Carousel` widgets.

The `ActionBar` comes with its own set of widgets, including the following (it's also possible to define your own `ActionItem` subclasses):

- `ActionCheck`
- `ActionButton`
- `ActionToggleButton`
- `ActionSeparator`
- `ActionGroup`
- `ActionOverflow`
- `ActionPrevious`

These classes are mostly self-explanatory, with the exception of the last three. `Action Previous` renders an icon and title into the left side of the action bar. In typical Android usage, touching this icon behaves like pressing the back button: it goes to the previous screen. However, this can be disabled by setting a `with_previous` setting. `Ac tionGroup` is just a drop-down "menu" in which you can put other `ActionItem` objects. `ActionOverflow` can explicitly contain other `ActionItems` as well. However, the neat thing about `ActionOverflow` is that if the `ActionBar` becomes too narrow, it will automatically move items into the `ActionOverflow` area so that they are still available in a drop-down. `ActionOverflow` is represented much like the menu icon on recent Android devices.

Example 8-9 shows the entire `ActionBar` on the `WeatherRoot` widget. It shows up in a `BoxLayout` above the `Carousel`. The Add Location and Settings buttons go inside an overflow, while the other buttons show up in the main view.

Example 8-9. Putting an ActionBar above the Carousel

```
<WeatherRoot>:
    carousel: carousel
    locations: locations
    current_weather: current_weather
    forecast: forecast
    BoxLayout:
        orientation: "vertical"
        ActionBar:
            ActionView:
                use_separator: True
                ActionPrevious:
                    title: "Kivy Weather"
                    with_previous: False
                ActionOverflow:
                    ActionButton:
                        text: "Add Location"
                        on_press: app.root.show_add_location_form()
                    ActionButton:
                        text: "Settings"
                        on_press: app.open_settings()
                ActionButton:
                    text: "Locations"
                    on_press: app.root.carousel.load_slide(app.root.locations)
                ActionButton:
                    text: "Current"
                    on_press: app.root.carousel.load_slide(app.root.current_weather)
                ActionButton:
                    text: "Forecast"
                    on_press: app.root.carousel.load_slide(app.root.forecast)
        Carousel:
            id: carousel
            Locations:
                id: locations
            CurrentWeather:
                id: current_weather
            Forecast:
                id: forecast
```

At this point, you can remove all the old `BoxLayout` and `Button` definitions that were showing up at the bottom of the other views. You'll probably want to leave the Cancel button on the Add Location form, though. This makes the source code a lot neater, and as you can see from Figure 8-2, the interface also looks a lot cleaner!

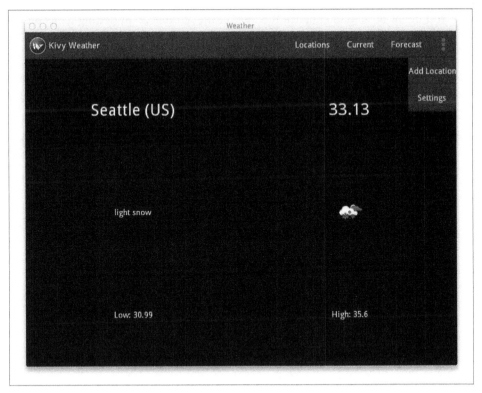

Figure 8-2. The ActionBar with the overflow area open

File It All Away

In this chapter, you did a fairly large code refactor and were introduced to three more advanced Kivy widgets—Carousel, ModalView, and ActionBar. Your application looks pretty good and might be considered production-ready. You'll test that theory in the next chapter, when you deploy it to your Android or iOS device.

In the meantime, here are a few additional things you might want to try to enhance your understanding:

- The location attribute on CurrentWeather and Forecast now seems somewhat redundant because those widgets are always updated at the same time, by show_cur rent_weather (which should probably be named change_location at this point). It might make more sense to store just one current_location on the Weather Root and have the child widgets access it from there.

- You might be able to enhance the look of the `ActionBar` by setting icons on the buttons. You could also put the metric/imperial switch directly into the `Action Bar` (as an `ActionCheck`) and do away with the settings overlay overhead.

- You could turn the `ActionBar` buttons into an `ActionToggle` to indicate which slide you are on. You'll need to listen to property changes on the `Carousel` to update the toggle button state when the slide changes.

- Consider the advantages and disadvantages of using `Popup` instead of `ModalView` for `AddLocationForm`.

- Take a look at the *kivy.uix* package for a wide variety of other useful Kivy widgets.

## CHAPTER 9

Releasing to Android and iOS

Now that you have a functional weather application, it's time to actually deploy it to your mobile device. In this chapter we'll discuss how to deploy to Android, which can be done from a Linux or Mac OS machine, and to iOS if both your host and device are Apple products. Kivy has a custom-built deployment tool called *Buildozer*. This tool is both a blessing and a curse. On the positive side, it works very hard (and very well) to take care of all the crazy dependencies that are required to deploy to these disparate platforms, and it has the second-coolest name in the packaging industry (Arch Linux's *pacman* package manager is number one). On the negative side, it can be difficult to debug when things go wrong and is another build system you have to learn. I find this frustrating, as I'm already familiar with so many other build tools--*setuptools*, *pip*, Make, Ant, *buildout*, Paver, and more. I'd have preferred to see Buildozer's features incorporated into the standard Python ecosystem. However, since they weren't and it's here and it works, I'm going to show you how to use it!

Getting Buildozer

Buildozer lives on Kivy's GitHub page (*https://github.com/kivy/buildozer*). It's currently alpha software, but it's far less cumbersome than older Kivy deployment methods, so I recommend you use it. I also recommend you use the master branch rather than one of the releases. The Kivy developers keep this project up-to-date with the ever-changing landscape of Android and iOS development, and it's rarely in a broken state. Unfortunately, however, Buildozer is not currently supported on Windows. In fact, there is no reliable way to deploy Kivy to Android devices from a Windows environment. The Kivy team provides a Linux virtual machine that you can run from inside your Windows box if you want to tackle deploying, but it's not a painless process.

If you have Git installed, which you should if you're serious about software development, the easiest way to install Buildozer is to clone the repository using the simple command `git clone https://github.com/kivy/buildozer.git`. I'd do this from whatever directory holds the code for your Kivy project so you can keep all your Kivy stuff in one place.

If you're just toying around and prefer not to install Git at this time, you can download a ZIP file directly from the Buildozer GitHub page (*https://github.com/kivy/buildoz er.git*). Click the Download ZIP button, which at the time of this writing appears in the right sidebar on the GitHub page, as shown in Figure 9-1.

Figure 9-1. The GitHub Download button

Once you've downloaded and extracted the Buildozer file, cd into the new *buildozer* directory and run the command python2 setup.py install. You may have to run this with sudo, depending on how your Python and operating system are set up.

Deploying Your Application

In this section, I'll focus on deploying your weather app to an Android device, as it's a bit simpler than for iOS. The iOS section will build on it, so you'll want to read both sections if you're an Apple user.

At the time of writing, even though Kivy supports Python 3, Buildozer is Python 2 only and installs a Python 2 environment onto your Android device. This means that if you have been developing in Python 3, you may have to make a couple of changes, which I have noted throughout the book, to get the application running on Android.

Namely, there is a call to super that needs to be changed to Python 2 format, and the clear method on the list needs to be replaced with an explicit del.

Buildozer works from a file named *buildozer.spec*, which allows you to describe and configure how your Kivy application will be deployed. Start by generating a default specification running the command buildozer init in the folder that contains your *main.py* and *weather.kv* files. Open the resulting *buildozer.spec* file in your text editor. You'll find that it contains a ton of settings, some of which are commented out, and all of which are described inside the file. Example 9-1 illustrates the changes I made to the default settings.

Example 9-1. Buildozer specification for an Android build

```
[app]

# (str) Title of your application ❶
title = Weather

# (str) Package name ❷
package.name = weather

# (str) Package domain (needed for android/ios packaging)
package.domain = org.example

# (str) Source code where the main.py live
source.dir = .

# (list) Source files to include (let empty to include all the files)
source.include_exts = py,png,jpg,kv,atlas

# (list) Source files to exclude (let empty to not exclude anything)
#source.exclude_exts = spec

# (list) List of directory to exclude (let empty to not exclude anything)
#source.exclude_dirs = tests, bin

# (list) List of exclusions using pattern matching
#source.exclude_patterns = license,images/*/*.jpg

# (str) Application versioning (method 1)
# version.regex = __version__ = '(.*)'
```

```
# version.filename = %(source.dir)s/main.py

# (str) Application versioning (method 2) ❸
version = 0.1

# (list) Application requirements ❹
requirements = kivy

# (str) Presplash of the application
#presplash.filename = %(source.dir)s/data/presplash.png

# (str) Icon of the application
#icon.filename = %(source.dir)s/data/icon.png

# (str) Supported orientation (one of landscape, portrait or all) ❺
orientation = all

# (bool) Indicate if the application should be fullscreen or not
fullscreen = 0


#
# Android specific   ❻
#

# (list) Permissions
android.permissions = INTERNET

# (int) Android API to use
android.api = 14

# (int) Minimum API required (8 = Android 2.2 devices)
android.minapi = 8

# (int) Android SDK version to use
android.sdk = 21

# (str) Android NDK version to use
android.ndk = 9

# (bool) Use --private data storage (True) or --dir public storage (False)
android.private_storage = True

# (str) Android NDK directory (if empty, it will be automatically downloaded.)
#android.ndk_path =

# (str) Android SDK directory (if empty, it will be automatically downloaded.)
#android.sdk_path =

# (str) Android entry point, default is ok for Kivy-based app
#android.entrypoint = org.renpy.android.PythonActivity
```

```
# (list) List of Java .jar files to add to the libs so that pyjnius can access
# their classes. Don't add jars that you do not need, since extra jars can slow
# down the build process. Allows wildcards matching, for example:
# OUYA-ODK/libs/*.jar
#android.add_jars = foo.jar,bar.jar,path/to/more/*.jar

# (list) List of Java files to add to the android project (can be java or a
# directory containing the files)
#android.add_src =

# (str) python-for-android branch to use, if not master, useful to try
# not yet merged features.
#android.branch = master

# (str) OUYA Console category. Should be one of GAME or APP
# If you leave this blank, OUYA support will not be enabled
#android.ouya.category = APP

# (str) Filename of OUYA Console icon. It must be a 732x412 png image.
#android.ouya.icon.filename = %(source.dir)s/data/ouya_icon.png

# (str) XML file to include as an intent filters in <activity> tag
#android.manifest.intent_filters =

# (list) Android additionnal libraries to copy into libs/armeabi
#android.add_libs_armeabi = libs/android/*.so

# (bool) Indicate whether the screen should stay on
# Don't forget to add the WAKE_LOCK permission if you set this to True
#android.wakelock = False

# (list) Android application meta-data to set (key=value format)
#android.meta_data =

# (list) Android library project to add (will be added in the
# project.properties automatically.)
#android.library_references =

#
# iOS specific
#

# (str) Name of the certificate to use for signing the debug version
# Get a list of available identities: buildozer ios list_identities
#ios.codesign.debug = "iPhone Developer: <lastname> <firstname> (<hexstring>)"

# (str) Name of the certificate to use for signing the release version
#ios.codesign.release = %(ios.codesign.debug)s


[buildozer]
```

```
# (int) Log level (0 = error only, 1 = info, 2 = debug (with command output)) ❼
log_level = 2


# --------------------------------------------------------------------------
# List as sections
#
# You can define all the "list" as [section:key].
# Each line will be considered as a option to the list.
# Let's take [app] / source.exclude_patterns.
# Instead of doing:
#
#     [app]
#     source.exclude_patterns = license,data/audio/*.wav,data/images/original/*
#
# This can be translated into:
#
#     [app:source.exclude_patterns]
#     license
#     data/audio/*.wav
#     data/images/original/*
#


# --------------------------------------------------------------------------
# Profiles
#
# You can extend section / key with a profile
# For example, you want to deploy a demo version of your application without
# HD content. You could first change the title to add "(demo)" in the name
# and extend the excluded directories to remove the HD content.
#
#     [app@demo]
#     title = My Application (demo)
#
#     [app:source.exclude_patterns@demo]
#     images/hd/*
#
# Then, invoke the command line with the "demo" profile:
#
#     buildozer --profile demo android debug
```

❶   Change the title to something meaningful.

❷   The package name should be unique to your dev environment. It will be concatenated to the package.domain, to create something that is globally unique.

❸ There are two ways to specify the version: scraping it from *main.py* or specifying it in *buildozer.spec*. The former is a better idea if your version number is referenced in multiple places, but since I'm only using the version for deploying, I specify it here. You have to remember to bump your version with each new release, or Google Play and the iTunes App Store won't pick it up.

❹ This is a list of third-party (nonstandard library) Python modules your app depends on. The weather app depends only on Kivy, but you can specify any other libraries you may require.

❺ The weather app can take advantage of autorotating.

❻ Uncomment several Android-specific options.

❼ Things will probably crash, so a debugging `log_level` is a good idea. Reset this before making your app public, or use the Buildozer Profiles feature.

Having updated this file to suit your fancy (you may want to add an icon, for example), you are almost ready to push it to your phone. The first thing you need to do is enable developer access on your phone, if it's running a recent version of Android. You might want to search the Web for how to do this on your specific device, but for recent versions of Android, it typically means finding the Build Number in the About menu (for me, it's buried inside About → Software information → More → Build Number) and tapping on it seven times. This is a strange, magical incantation, but eventually it'll tell you that you've unlocked developer options on your phone. You'll then need to find the "Developer options" menu and enable USB Debugging.

The next step is to run the command `buildozer android debug deploy run`. You can easily tell what this command is supposed to do, but it will probably fail multiple times before you get it running. If it fails, edit the *buildozer.spec* file. Find the section titled `[buildozer]` toward the end of the file and change the `log_level` setting to 2 for debugging. Next time you run Buildozer, it will give you informative errors telling you that you are missing dependencies. I personally had to install a ton of packages, including Cython, virtualenv, g++, Ant, and a Java compiler before it would run. However, on the fourth attempt, it managed to complete after taking *ages* to download all the Android dependencies (don't do this on a rate-limited 3G network!), compile them, compile the *.apk*, upload it to the phone, and, eventually, open it on the phone. Go grab a coffee. Assuming the app is working, when you get back you should be able to interact with it just as you did when it was running on your desktop.

Of course, it's not safe to assume everything is working. Android has a variety of useful debugging tools that you can use to debug your application. I can't describe them all here, but I'll discuss a couple that I think are absolutely vital.

Buildozer provides the `logcat` command, which calls `adb logcat` under the hood (you may already be familiar with Android Debug Bridge, or `adb`). You can run it with `buildozer android logcat`. This command provides all sorts of diagnostic information in the terminal. Most importantly, you can see any Python or Java tracebacks related to your program. Try running `buildozer run` in a different terminal while the log is being displayed. You'll see the Kivy logging info pop up, and if you've got a Python error in your program, you'll see the traceback.

Another tool that is useful (more for prototyping and experimenting than for debugging) is the Kivy Remote Shell. You can access it from Kivy's GitHub page (*http://bit.ly/remoteshell*) using Git or by downloading the ZIP file as you did with Buildozer. Kivy Remote Shell ships with a Buildozer spec file. Once you have cloned it, you simply have to run `buildozer android debug deploy run` to get the Kivy Remote Shell installed.

But what is the Kivy Remote Shell? It's kind of the Python shell equivalent of `adb log cat`. You can run the app on your phone and then connect to it from a computer on the same wireless network using `ssh` (`ssh` is preinstalled on most Linux and Mac OS systems; on Windows, you'll want to look up a program called PuTTY). The exact command you need to enter to log in to the device is displayed on the phone's screen. You'll be asked for a password, which is `kivy`. Once you've logged in, you'll be presented with a Python prompt that you can use to control code on the phone. The `app` object is available, and you can add Kivy widgets to the window using `app.root.add_widget`. This is useful for seeing how layouts look on the phone, but I mostly use it for experimenting with `pyjnius`, the Python-to-Java bridge that can be used for manipulating Java Android classes on a phone.

Finally, the absolute best tool for Kivy debugging is called Internet Relay Chat (IRC). If you're having trouble getting Buildozer working, get in touch with the Kivy team using IRC or the Kivy mailing list. Some of the tools discussed in this chapter are still alpha, and bug reports from people who are willing to help the developers understand the problems are the most important means of turning them into the solid software that is the rest of Kivy.

In Which the Author Digresses

I have a strong aversion to having separate interfaces for developers and so-called "normal" users. I believe this creates a culture of inequality. The unbelievable arrogance of the software engineer who decided that normal users needed to be protected from developer options is disturbing and disheartening. This engineer was clearly a "deatheater" who thinks the "muggles" of the world need to be kept further in the dark, rather than enlightened.

The world is coming to entirely depend on technology, and we need to welcome the inexperienced users, make them feel comfortable, help them become adept, and, if we are lucky, prompt them to become new developers themselves. The generation of children who grew up on locked-down tablets and mobile phones never had a chance to explore and experiment, to break and fix things. If you have kids, buy them a Raspberry Pi to prevent another generation from missing the chance for free learning. Assuming that your users cannot handle the systems you give them is the most horrible disservice you can do them.

This does not mean that interfaces should not be intuitive and easy to use. A system that is easy to use should be equally accessible for experienced power users and new users. Setting sensible defaults, using convention over configuration, and implementing other paradigms can ease this process. But the developer culture must stop enforcing user ignorance.

Deploying to iOS

Unlike Android, Apple's draconian development policies require that you have an Apple developer license before you can test or debug your application on an iOS device. This allows Apple to ensure the quality of the applications available for these devices. For normal iOS development, Apple provides access to an emulator tool, but for Kivy, you'll probably want to test on a real device. If you don't already have a developer license, follow the instructions on the Apple developer website (*http://bit.ly/a-developer*) to get one.

Once you've paid your dues and logged in to the Apple development center, you can download and install XCode if you don't have it already. Run XCode and plug in your iOS device. The XCode Device Organizer should pop up automatically. Select the iOS device from the menu and click the "Use for Development" button. You will be prompted for an Apple ID that is associated with a development account. You will then be invited to request a certificate for the device. Follow this process and confirm that the certificate shows up in your Apple Developer Account in the web browser.

That should be all the extra work you need to do to get permission to develop from Apple. You can now return to the Kivy development process. Create a *buildozer.spec* file similar to Example 9-1 (if you are deploying to both Android and iOS, you can use the same *buildozer.spec* file). You can ignore the Android section this time, but you'll need to add a string to the "iOS specific" section. This string is constructed from the certificate you just created, and can be tricky to get right. Luckily, Buildozer has a command to do this for you: `buildozer ios list_identities`. If your XCode is set up and your iOS device is connected, you should get output like Example 9-2.

Example 9-2. Output of buildozer ios list_identities

```
1) <LONG HEX STRING> "iPhone Developer: Your Full Name (<HEXSTRING>)"
  1 valid identities found
Available identities:
  - "iPhone Developer: Your Full Name (<HEXSTRING>)"
```

Copy the contents of the quoted string under "Available identities" into the "iOS specific" section of your *buildozer.spec* file, remembering to uncomment both `ios.codesign` lines. See Example 9-3 (other than this section, the file is unmodified from Example 9-1).

Example 9-3. Buildozer specification for an iOS build

```
#
# iOS specific
#

# (str) Name of the certificate to use for signing the debug version
# Get a list of available identities: buildozer ios list_identities
ios.codesign.debug = "iPhone Developer: Dustin Phillips (XAQ2M755YE)"

# (str) Name of the certificate to use for signing the release version
ios.codesign.release = %(ios.codesign.debug)s
```

Now you can run the command `buildozer ios debug deploy run`, similarly to the Android deployment. If all goes well, your Kivy app should run cleanly on your iOS device.

Buildozer Dependencies on Mac OS

The first time I ran Buildozer on my Mac, it complained about some missing packages, including `pkgconfig`, `autoconf`, and `automake`. You may have to do some research to figure out how to install these if you don't already have them. You will have the best luck using `homebrew` or `macports`, very useful tools if you do much Unix programming.

Alternatively, you can manually download and install packages with typical Unix commands (available if you have XCode installed). For example, I had to download the latest version of `pkg-config` (*http://bit.ly/ix-releases*) and install it using the typical Unix process:

```
./configure --with-internal-glib
make
sudo make install
```

Unfortunately, I can't guess which dependencies you might need to install or already have available. Dependency management is an integral part of programming, and you'll have to get good at it for whichever operating system you choose to use. Normally, the Buildozer process will fail with a clean error message telling you what you need to install, but it won't tell you how. Stack overflow and a web search are definitely your friends here.

For debugging, you can open XCode and view the logging output from the device, similar to what you see when you run the `logcat` command on Android. The command `buildozer xcode` will open the actual XCode project associated with your Kivy project.

Android Bonus: Accessing the GPS

Before I get into this section, I want to apologize to iOS users for not including them. The Kivy team has developed an API for accessing native features (including the accelerometer, camera, GPS, and notifications) on a variety of operating systems. Sadly, like Buildozer, the library is still in alpha as I write this, and the only feature supported on iOS is the accelerometer. The good news is that you can use this API with your Android device, and once the Kivy team adds support for iOS devices, your code should run virtually unmodified. The even better news is that all Kivy libraries are completely open source, and the team would be delighted to receive a pull request if you add iOS support for their API.

If you aren't currently deploying to an Android device, you can skip to the next section.

The Kivy team has created an awesome library called pyjnius that allows you to access Java classes from inside Python. This is how they provide all the Kivy goodness on Android. There is a similar library for accessing Objective-C classes on iOS called pyobjus. Both of these are very powerful, but they require a deep knowledge of the underlying classes being accessed. Fortunately, the Kivy team has also created a platform-independent API called plyer that wraps these features in an easy-to-use and consistent Python API.

The plyer library (*https://github.com/kivy/plyer.git*) is not bundled with Kivy, so you'll need to install it yourself. You can do this through Git or by downloading the ZIP file as you did with Buildozer. The command python setup.py install should install it for you.

The next step is to hook up the Current Location button on the Add Location form to a method that knows how to use the GPS. Example 9-4 illustrates.

Example 9-4. Callback for the Current Location button

```
Button:
    text: "Current Location"
    size_hint_x: 25
    on_press: root.current_location()
```

Of course, this will just crash the app if you don't actually add the method being called. You'll need a few new imports first, as shown in Example 9-5.

Example 9-5. Imports for accessing the GPS

```
from plyer import gps
from kivy.clock import Clock, mainthread
from kivy.uix.popup import Popup
from kivy.uix.label import Label
```

The method itself, along with a stub callback, is displayed in Example 9-6.

Example 9-6. Start accessing the GPS and show a pop-up if it's not available

```python
def current_location(self):
    try:
        gps.configure(on_location=self.on_location)
        gps.start()
    except NotImplementedError:
      popup = Popup(title="GPS Error",
          content=Label(text="GPS support is not implemented on your platform")
            ).open()
        Clock.schedule_once(lambda d: popup.dismiss(), 3)

@mainthread
def on_location(self, **kwargs):
    print(kwargs)
```

The `@mainthread` decorator essentially wraps the method in a `Clock.schedule_once` call so that it always runs on the main Kivy thread. Depending on the underlying implementation, the `plyer` GPS module may be executed in a background thread that isn't allowed to access the Kivy main loop.

I tested this first on my Linux laptop, for which GPS is not supported. As expected, the pop-up is displayed for three seconds and then disappears. The next step is to check it out on the Android phone. However, before you can do that, you need to add the `plyer` requirement and a couple of permissions to your *buildozer.spec* file, as shown in Example 9-7 and Example 9-8.

Example 9-7. Accessing GPS permissions

```
# (list) Permissions
android.permissions = INTERNET,ACCESS_FINE_LOCATION,ACCESS_COARSE_LOCATION
```

Example 9-8. Depending on plyer

```
# (list) Application requirements
requirements = kivy,plyer
```

If you now run `buildozer android debug deploy run logcat`, your app should pop up on the phone, and when you click the Current Location button on the Add Location form, you should get some output on the console. Now all you need to do is implement the `on_location` function to look up the user's current location on Open Weather Map. Luckily, Open Weather Map has an API to request by latitude and longitude. We could request the weather details that way, but as you can see in Example 9-9, I cheated and just grabbed the location from the response. Then I pass this into the `show_cur rent_weather` method, and presto, everything works!

Example 9-9. Looking up the location on Open Weather Map

```python
@mainthread
def on_location(self, **kwargs):
```

```
search_template = "http://api.openweathermap.org/data/2.5/" +
    "weather?lat={}&lon={}"
search_url = search_template.format(kwargs['lat'], kwargs['lon'])
data = requests.get(search_url).json()
location = (data['sys']['country'], data['name'])
WeatherApp.get_running_app().root.show_current_weather(location)
```

Run buildozer android debug deploy run again. If you hit up the Add Location form and touch Current Weather, it should locate you (if your GPS is on) and search for the weather wherever you are.

Keeping It Running

You'll notice that as soon as the screen turns off, your Kivy app exits, and it restarts when you turn it on again. This isn't a horrible thing for a weather application, but it's not exactly desirable. Luckily, Kivy supports a so-called pause mode that allows you to keep the window open. All you have to do is add an on_pause method to the WeatherApp class that returns True instead of the default False. See Example 9-10.

Example 9-10. Enabling pause on mobile

```
def on_pause(self):
    return True
```

Deploy it to your phone using Buildozer, and you can switch back and forth between your Kivy app and other applications with ease.

File It All Away

Your Kivy app is functionally complete! It runs on your Android or iOS phone, and you have app files (they live in the *bin* directory) that can be submitted to the Google Play Market or iTunes App Store. In my experience, a program is never finished. However, I have to stop somewhere, so there are several things I will leave you to explore on your own before you build a totally new App in the next chapter:

- The plyer library provides access to the accelerometer. You could create a "shake to change from forecast to current weather" feature.

- plyer also has a notification system that you can integrate in a few different ways.

- If you have Android or iOS experience (or if you want to get some), see if you can figure out how to access other features of the underlying OS using pyjnius or pyobjus.

- Use the app for a few days and fix any pain points you discover while using it.

- Write another Kivy app from scratch. And another and another!

That's it for the weather application, though I'm sure you'll find many ways to improve it as you use it. In the next chapters, you'll be looking at a completely different kind of Kivy application, a mobile game.

## CHAPTER 10

Writing a Simple Mobile Game

Now that you've written and deployed your first mobile app, I hope you're raring to build another one! I actually recommend that your second mobile application be something that you develop on your own. However, once you've dabbled in that for a bit, come back here, and I'll show you how to build a rather silly game. One of the primary complaints about Kivy is that the widgets don't integrate well with the "native" look and feel on the various platforms on which it runs. This complaint rarely applies to gaming, and Kivy is a perfect mobile-gaming platform.

In this chapter, I'll describe a simple idea for a game that has been bouncing around in my head. I'll start you on some basic touch interaction and graphics. In the next chapter, you'll look at adding enemies and scoring to the game. Finally, you'll finish the game by adding graphic textures.

Designing a Game

Over the course of my career, I've implemented a few games, but I don't consider myself a game designer. In fact, I can't promise that the game you are about to implement is going to be fun or even playable. However, the legendary Flappy Bird[1] game tells us that in the mobile space, games don't have to be fun or playable to be successful!

The gameplay I have in mind is, I hope, quite simple, both to explain and to implement. Here's the interaction that I'm picturing:

- An entity (representing your character, the "good guy") in the center of the screen grows when the player touches the screen and shrinks when she releases.

---

1. A notoriously frustrating and difficult game that was above all, extremely popular before the author unexpectedly pulled it from the market.

- "Enemies" will periodically come in from offscreen and flow toward the center of the screen.
- If the character is growing when touched by an entity, it scores a point; otherwise the game is over.
- Growing the character causes energy to be expended, while shrinking it recovers energy at a slower rate.
- If the character shrinks to its minimum size, energy is recovered more quickly.
- If too much energy is expended, it is impossible for the character to grow or to protect itself from an enemy.
- To give the player incentive to take risks, enemies that are killed further from the center are worth more points than ones caught when the character is smaller.

In this chapter, you'll implement the growing and shrinking character; I'll visit the enemies and characters in later chapters.

Notice that I've designed gameplay without describing a theme for the game. I think it's generally a good idea to get the mechanics down before going too far with animation; Angry Birds could just as easily have been a game about happy crickets without changing the underlying mechanics whatsoever.

The game being designed here could be set in the Old West or underwater and have the same basic engine. Designing a theme, story, and graphics for a game is a complex process, but it's not strictly pertinent to the coding aspect I'll be discussing in this book.

I won't be covering graphics at all until the next chapter, but to set some context for the code you're about to write, I want to have a theme in place. Even though it's rather cliche, this game is going to have a space theme. You'll see your circular spaceship traveling on a starry background with enemies coming directly at it, kind of like a gravity well. I figure this will allow me to be a bit less selective about the graphics on the grounds that nobody can argue about how a futuristic space enemy is supposed to look!

Finally, you need to come up with a name for your game. Once again, I'll demonstrate my lack of marketing skills by choosing the name, *Conservation Of Energy*. The game app will be called `EnergyApp` for short.

To get started with your new Kivy app, create a new folder named `energy`. Inside that folder, create a new empty *main.py* file and an empty `energy.kv` file. See if you can remember how to get a basic Kivy app up and running after all this time (hint: it's four lines of code in *main.py*). See Chapter 1 if you need a refresher.

Float Layouts

For the WeatherApp, you mostly used BoxLayout to position elements relative to each other. For this game, we will be defining the positions of various components ourselves, mostly using basic math relative to the size of the window. Therefore, the root widget in the KV language file will be a FloatLayout.

FloatLayout places zero restrictions on the location of its child widgets. This shifts a lot of control (and responsibility) to you, the coder. It can essentially operate in one of two modes: *hint mode* and *absolute mode*. Hint mode allows you to set the size_hint and pos_hint properties such that the widget's size and position are relative to percentages of the parent window. In absolute mode, the size_hint and pos_hint are set to None, and you set the pos and size properties manually. Hints and absolute positioning are independent in all dimensions and can therefore be combined in curious ways. For example, you can use a size_hint in the x dimension and an absolute size in the y dimension. Or you can mix a size_hint with an absolute position. The KV Language file in Example 10-1 illustrates several of these combinations.

Example 10-1. Absolute and hint positioning in FloatLayouts

```
FloatLayout:
    Button:
        size_hint: None, None
        pos_hint: {}
        size: 200, 20
        pos: 30, 30
        text: "abs size, abs pos"
    Button:
        size_hint: .15, .08
        pos_hint: {"x": 0.1, "y": 0.1}
        text: "hint size, hint pos"
    Button:
        size_hint: .15, .09
        pos_hint: {}
        pos: 100, 100
        text: "hint size, abs pos"
    Button:
        size_hint: None, None
        pos_hint: {"x": 0.18, "y": 0.28}
        size: 300, 20
        text: "abs size, hint Pos"
    Button:
        size_hint: .3, None
        height: 20
        pos_hint: {'x': 0.2}
        y: 200
        text: "hint width, abs height, hint x, abs y"
```

Note that there are no rules with FloatLayout. Widgets can take up the same space. They can overlap or totally obscure other widgets. They can be positioned entirely outside the view or have no size at all.

When you use absolute sizing and positioning, the widgets always show up at the same location (measured from the lower-left corner), regardless of the size and shape of the window. Hints, on the other hand, use percentages of the parent size, so if you resize the window, the widget sizes and positions will change. The KV file is rendered in two different sized screens in Figure 10-1 and Figure 10-2.

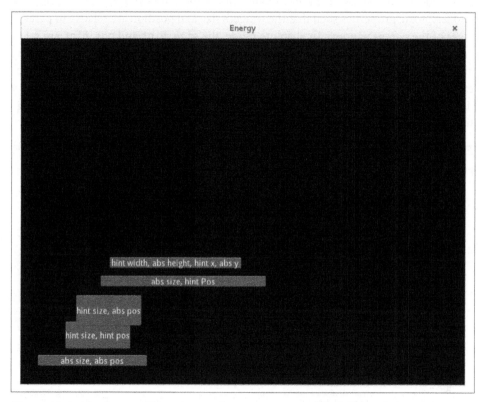

Figure 10-1. Absolute and hint sizes and positions in a wide window

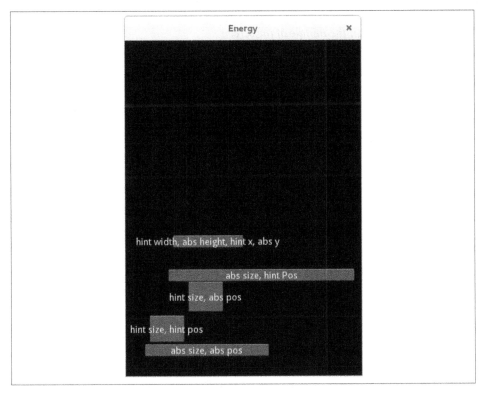

Figure 10-2. Absolute and hint sizes and positions in a narrow window

With this knowledge about the power of FloatLayout, you are ready to use one to position your ship, and later enemies, on the screen.

The Ship Widget

Start by creating a Ship widget. This will represent the main character, a mysterious object that grows when you touch the screen and shrinks when you release your touch.[2]

Make a Dot

The first step is to render a dot of a fixed size in the center of the screen. This sentence says a lot about how to position the object relative to a FloatLayout. The words "fixed size" suggest that size_hint should be disabled, while the "center of the screen" indicates that a pos_hint will be useful for positioning. Have a look at Example 10-2.

---

2. Nobody said the ship had to obey any laws of physics in *this* universe.

Example 10-2. A dot in the middle of the screen

```
FloatLayout:
    Ship:

<Ship@Widget>:
    size_hint: None, None  # ❶
    width: "20dp"
    height: self.width  # ❷
    pos_hint:  # ❸
        {
        "center_x": 0.5,
        "center_y": 0.5
        }
    canvas:  # ❹
        Color:
            rgba: 1, 1, 1, 1
        Ellipse:
            pos: self.pos
            size: self.size
```

❶ Disable size hinting in both dimensions

❷ Set the height to be equal to the width so we always get a square bounding box (and therefore always draw a circle inside it.) That way, to change the size of the circle, you only need to set the width property. However, this means that your code must responsibly never set the height to something else.

❸ The pos_hint property takes a dictionary where keys can be any of x, y, right, top, center_x, and center_y. In general, you should only pick one from the x dimension and one from the y dimension. In this case, set both center_x and center_y to 0.5, indicating that the center of the dot should show up in the center of its parent FloatLayout.

❹ Canvas instructions are able to refer to the self.size and self.pos to render graphics. Note that even though pos_hint was used in the preceding code, self.pos has a valid value. The layout sets pos based on the pos_hint; they aren't strictly independent values. The same can be said for size_hint, which is why layouts require you to explicitly set size_hint to None if you want to manipulate the size directly.

As Figure 10-3 shows, the rendering of this code is not very exciting. But the possibilities! Think of the endless possibilities!

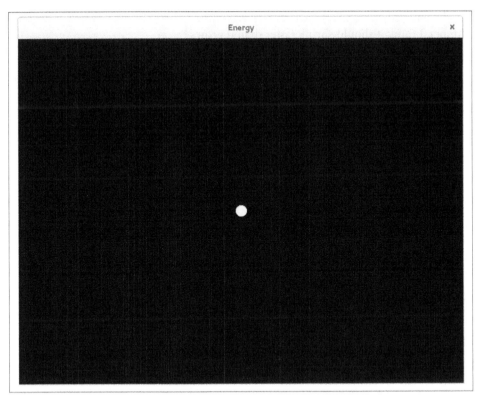

Figure 10-3. See the dot in the middle of the screen

Make the Dot Grow

The next step is to make this dot grow when the screen is touched and shrink when you release the finger. You dealt with touch events in Chapter 7 and animations using the Kivy clock in Chapter 5. That's all you need to define a basic touch interactive widget!

First, remove the @Widget reference from *energy.kv* so that the Ship class can be defined and manipulated in *main.py* instead. The new class should have a NumericProperty named growth. This property represents the number of display pixels that the widget should grow each section. If the widget is shrinking, then this number will be negative.

You'll also need a min_width property so that you know when to stop shrinking the widget. It should be set to 20 display pixels, and the *energy.kv* file can set the initial width to the value of this property instead of hardcoding the display pixels.

You might expect the touch down and up events to actively change the size of the dot. However, you don't know how long the user is going to hold his finger down. Instead, these events only need to set the growth property to an appropriate positive or negative number. I think it should shrink faster than it grows.[3]

Of course, if you're not changing the dot sizes in the touch events, you need to do it somewhere. That's where the Kivy Clock comes in. Use it to schedule an update method to be called every tenth of a second. This method is the one that changes the size of the dot depending on a combination of the growth property and the amount of time that has elapsed since it was last called.

Example 10-3 shows all these moving parts in one code snippet.

Example 10-3. Code for growing a dot when a touch event happens

```
from kivy.app import App
from kivy.uix.widget import Widget
from kivy.properties import NumericProperty
from kivy.metrics import dp  # ❶
from kivy.clock import Clock


class Ship(Widget):
    growth = NumericProperty(0)  # ❷
    min_size = NumericProperty(dp(20))  # ❸

    def __init__(self, **kwargs):
        super(Ship, self).__init__(**kwargs)
        Clock.schedule_interval(self.update, 0.1)  # ❹

    def on_touch_down(self, event):
        self.growth = dp(8)   # ❺

    def on_touch_up(self, event):
        self.growth = dp(-16)

    def update(self, delta):  # ❻
        self.width += self.growth * delta  # ❼
        if self.width <= self.min_size:  # ❽
            self.width = self.min_size
            self.growth = 0


class EnergyApp(App):
    pass

if __name__ == '__main__':
    EnergyApp().run()
```

3. I implemented a prototype of this before I started writing. I came up with most of the hardcoded numbers I'm throwing at you by trial and error. This is a good way to figure out works in game design. Then if you can get a mathematical definition of either "fun" or "addictive," you might be more likely to top the Android market!

❶ I'm being careful to distinguish between *display pixels* and *real pixels* because many modern devices have very dense displays with tiny pixels. An app that looks fine on your laptop might look tiny on your phone or tablet. Kivy's *display pixels* are a platform-independent unit of measure; they should look the same on all devices. In KV language, you can use a string with the suffix dp to represent display pixels. But in Python files, you are better off calling the dp() function to convert display pixels to the real pixel value used on the underlying platform.

❷ growth is the number of real pixels that the circle is growing or shrinking each second.

❸ min_size is the number of real pixels that the dot should be at rest; it should not shrink smaller than this value.

❹ When the Ship is constructed, hook up its update() method to be called approximately every tenth of a second.

❺ Set growth to eight display pixels. The dp function may convert this to a much higher number on displays with high pixel densities.

❻ When Clock calls update(), it passes in the number of seconds since the method was last called. This value should be around 0.1, but it won't be exact due to hardware performance.

❼ Therefore, multiply the per-second growth by the delta to get the exact number of real pixels that should be added to the width.

❽ If the circle has shrunk to less than its minimum size, then reset it to the minimum size and stop shrinking by setting growth to zero.

This is a surprisingly concise amount of code considering the effect. As with all animations, it's hard to show the result in a book, but Figure 10-4 should give you an idea.

Adding Energy

The next step is to add the concept of energy to the character. If the character has energy, then it can grow; but when it runs out of energy, it will stop growing. You could choose any value for the total amount of available energy; the important thing is that there is a range. Since the amount of energy is easily thought of as a percentage, I'm going to make it a float value ranging between 0.0 and 1.0.

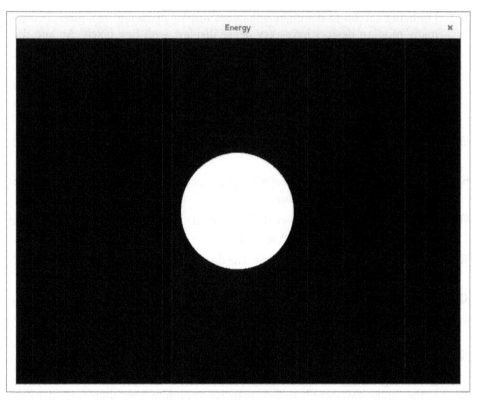

Figure 10-4. The dot after it has grown for some time

Visually, there are several ways that the amount of available energy could be rendered. The following options come to mind:

- Render an energy bar somewhere else on the screen.
- Change the color of the dot for different energy levels.
- Use the dot's transparency to show available energy.
- Show an arc on the dot to indicate energy as a percentage.

All of these are workable options, and I've experimented with several of them. For this chapter, I'm going to go with the arc idea. A full circle shows that maximum energy is available, a half circle shows half energy, and no arc indicates that energy has been exhausted.

Recording Energy

First, add some properties to the dot widget to record the current energy level and, akin to the size-growth property, the amount that it is increasing or decreasing per second. See Example 10-4.

Example 10-4. Adding properties for available energy

```
energy = NumericProperty(1.0)
energy_growth = NumericProperty(0)
```

Now adjust the two touch events so that a reasonable energy_growth value is selected when the character is growing or shrinking, as shown in Example 10-5.

Example 10-5. Touch events now have energy

```
def on_touch_down(self, event):
    self.energy_growth = -0.05
    self.growth = dp(8)

def on_touch_up(self, event):
    self.energy_growth = 0.03
    self.growth = dp(-16)
```

The tricky part, now, is to adjust the total available energy on each update cycle and then to determine whether to adjust either energy or growth rate if certain conditions have been met. While I was testing this, I printed the value of self.growth, self.size, self.energy, and self.energy_growth to the console inside the update method. That way I could see how the numbers interacted when the touch events happened. The comments in the end result in Example 10-6 explain the conclusions I came to, but I want to reiterate that this piece of code came largely from the tried-and-tested technique known as trial and error.

Different developers code in different ways. While I did use trial and error to build the conditionals in Example 10-6, you might prefer to reason through the entire set of conditionals before typing any code.

I don't actually use trial and error here, exactly. Rather, I used code to document my reasoning process until all the possible cases had been covered. Loosely, I came up with most of the comments separating each piece of logic, then figured out the relatively simple if statements for each one. As I figured out one case, I may have noticed that other comments needed to be added and conditionals defined for them.

Example 10-6. Full update method with growth and energy calculations

```
def update(self, delta):
    # Adjust size and energy if their growth is non-zero
```

```
        self.width += self.growth * delta
        self.energy += self.energy_growth * delta

        # Ran out of energy: stop growing or consuming energy
        if self.energy <= 0 and self.growth > 0:
            self.energy = 0
            self.growth = 0
            self.energy_growth = 0
        # Shrinking has passed minimum size: stop shrinking
        if self.width <= self.min_size:
            self.width = self.min_size
            self.growth = 0
            # Energy rises faster when no longer shrinking
            self.energy_growth = 0.06
        # Energy has finsihed regenerating: stop generating
        if self.energy >= 1:
            self.energy = 1
            self.energy_growth = 0

    print("")
    print(self.energy)
    print(self.energy_growth)
    print(self.width)
    print(self.growth)
```

Displaying Energy

It's one thing to measure and store the amount of available energy, but the game will seem very mysterious unless the user can also see a representation of that number. I want to display the available energy as a continuous arc. This is easier to do in the *energy.kv* file than the Python file, since it involves graphics instructions. The arc gets drawn on the same `canvas` as the dot itself.

As I was coding this, I had the idea[4] that the color of the arc could further indicate whether or not the character is currently safe from soon-to-arrive enemies. The definition of safe is: *if the character is currently growing, it is safe to bump into enemies (its shields are active). If it is shrinking or at its minimum size, touching enemies will kill it.* The canvas instructions in Example 10-7 create an appropriately sized and colored arc.

Example 10-7. Rendering the amount of energy left and character safety

```
canvas:
    Color:
        rgba: 1, 1, 1, 1
    Ellipse:
        pos: self.pos
        size: self.size
```

---

4. Another indication that I never think things through before I start coding. Coding helps me think.

```
Color:
    rgba:  ❶
        (
        [.3, .4, 1, 1]
        if self.growth > 0 else
        [1, .4, .3, 1]
        )
Line:
    width: 2
    circle:  ❷
        [
        self.center_x,
        self.center_y,
        (self.width / 2) - dp(5),
        360 * self.energy,
        0
        ]
```

❶ Remember that the value of a property can be arbitrary Python. The value for
   the color uses the Python ternary operator (essentially x if True else y) split
   across several lines. If the character is currently growing, then it renders as blue;
   otherwise it renders as red.

❷ Drawing a line of width 2 is pretty straightforward, as you saw in Chapter 5.
   Rather than passing points here, you are instead using Line's circle parameter,
   which basically uses algebra to calculate the equation for a circle of given inputs.

The circle parameter passed into line is rather interesting. It takes the following arguments, in order:

- center_x to indicate the center of the circle
- center_y to use the center of the widget itself
- radius to show the radius circle; half the size of the widget with five display pixels
  of margin
- arc_start to show the start location of the arc in degrees (0 to 360)
- arc_end to show the end location of the arc

I chose to make the start location 360; the end location is the percentage of degrees left
if you multiply by the amount of energy. This causes a full circle to open up in a coun-
terclockwise direction. (See Figure 10-5).

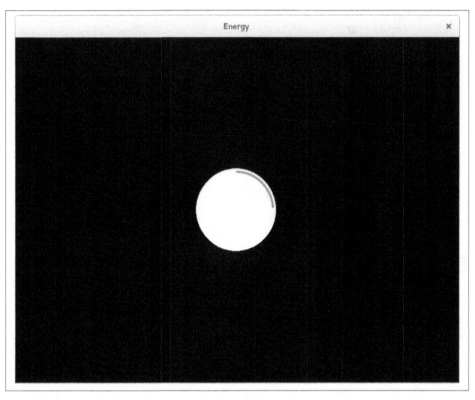

Figure 10-5. About three-quarters of the energy has been used

File It All Away

Since you wrapped up one application in the last chapter, this one started you on a brand-new one, a basic mobile game. You learned how to use a `FloatLayout` and then proceeded to build most of the interaction around the main character in your game.

Since this is a game, you can really let your imagination run wild with the game mechanics. Here are some ideas to get you started:

- Toy with the `schedule_interval` call to see what happens if you do updates more or less frequently.

- I hardcoded a lot of values (such as the growth factors). Pull these "magic numbers" into a set of constants to make them easier to read. Then see how the touch interaction changes if you tweak them.

- I haven't discussed multitouch at all, but if you search the Kivy documentation and examples, you'll find some great examples of it. How could you change the game by adding another touch?

- There are a lot of conditionals in the update() method, and you can likely imagine that a more complicated game would have many more of these. Can you think of other ways to structure game logic so that it is easy to maintain and comprehend?

This dot that grows with energy is not exactly riveting. It is a fun game to play... for about 14 seconds. In the next chapter, you'll add enemies and scoring to the mix, giving your players a goal and some risk/reward tradeoffs.

## CHAPTER 11

Modeling Enemies

The "game" as it stands is probably more fun for you to play, since you wrote it, than for anyone else. Truth be told, it's kind of boring. What it needs is a little anxiety, a thrill of the chase, and a way to keep score.

The behavior of enemies should be relatively straightforward. Each one will start somewhere off the screen and then drift toward the character in the center at a constant rate of speed. Eventually, the growing character and the moving enemy collide. Depending on whether the character is safe or not, the enemies' points will be absorbed by the player, or the player will die. The enemy will also have a score associated with it; the farther it is from the center of the screen, the higher the score.

Periodic Random Enemies

The enemy will be a FloatLayout with some basic graphics and a label with the current score. Start by creating this class in *main.py*. As shown in Example 11-1, you should put a couple properties on the class. The first represents the current score the player can achieve by killing this enemy. Later you'll set this score depending on the distance the enemy is from the center. The second is the velocity at which the enemy is approaching you. We'll discuss why the velocity is a list of two values shortly.

You'll need to import the base class using from kivy.uix.floatlayout import Float Layout, and the ListProperty using from kivy.properties import ListProperty.

Example 11-1. Enemy class with a score property

```
class Enemy(FloatLayout):
    score = NumericProperty(0)
    velocity = ListProperty([0, 0])
```

The next step is to have enemies show up on the screen at some random interval. In the final version, the enemies will show up outside the screen and drift inward. However,

I'm going to focus on having them show up statically at some point inside the screen first. That way, I can see how they look while I work out the styling for them in the KV language file.

The code that generates new enemies should live on the EnergyApp class. When that class is initialized, make it schedule a call to make_enemy on the Clock. See Example 11-2 for all the details.

Example 11-2. Scheduling enemy creation

```
class EnergyApp(App):
    enemy_rate = NumericProperty(5)    ❶
    score = NumericProperty(0)    ❷

    def __init__(self):
        super(EnergyApp, self).__init__()
        self.schedule_next_enemy()

    def schedule_next_enemy(self):    ❸
        Clock.schedule_once(
            self.make_enemy,
            random.random() * self.enemy_rate    ❹
        )

    def make_enemy(self, delta):
        pos = (    ❺
            random.randint(0, self.root.width),
            random.randint(0, self.root.height)
        )
        enemy = Enemy(pos=pos)
        self.root.add_widget(enemy)
        self.schedule_next_enemy()
```

❶ The maximum number of seconds between enemies showing up. This could conceivably be decreased as the game progresses.

❷ I reckon we'll need to keep track of the player's score at some point, so why not add the property now?

❸ This method simply tells the Clock to schedule creation of a new enemy in a random number of seconds. I split this code out into a method because it is called from two places, and it seems like the kind of thing that might be changed in the future. It would not be good if it got changed in one place but not the other. Also, it makes the calling code more readable, since it's immediately obvious what schedule_next_enemy is supposed to do, but less obvious what the Clock.schedule... construct does.

❹ Remember to import random.

❺ As mentioned in the text, this is just temporary so you can see where enemies pop up while you style the widget in the KV language.

That's all the logic you need to create enemies, but since there is nothing being rendered in the FloatLayout, they'll be as invisible and noninteractive as a neutrino. Adding some KV styling will fix this.

Styling an Enemy

The KV language rule for the Enemy class doesn't have to be too complicated to start with. A simple dot with a Label on it to indicate the enemy's current score is sufficient. See Example 11-3.

Example 11-3. KV language to style an enemy.

```
<Enemy>:
    size_hint: None, None
    width: "20dp"
    height: self.width
    canvas.before:
        Color:
            rgba: .7, .2, .1, 1
        Ellipse:
            pos: self.pos
            size: self.size
    Label:
        pos: root.pos
        size: self.texture_size
        text: str(root.score)
```

There is nothing you haven't seen before in this example. It uses canvas.before to draw the Ellipse so that the Label shows up in front of it.

If you run this code for a few tens of seconds, it will look something like Figure 11-1.

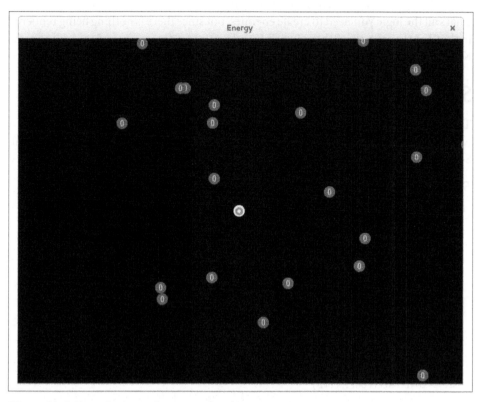

Figure 11-1. Enemies, enemies everywhere!

Positioning Enemies Outside the Screen

Now that you've seen the enemies, you should move them to their appropriate location. They should pop up outside the screen. There are several ways to do this. My first thought was to use random x and y coordinates greater than some value, but this would cause enemies to bunch up at the corners, as shown in Figure 11-2.

One reason for this is the rectangular form factor of the phone. However, this problem would still exist even if the screen were square.[1] I think it would make more sense to have enemies show up in a random circle just outside the width of the phone, as shown in Figure 11-3

---

1. There would be other problems in that case, like trying to fit it in your hand.

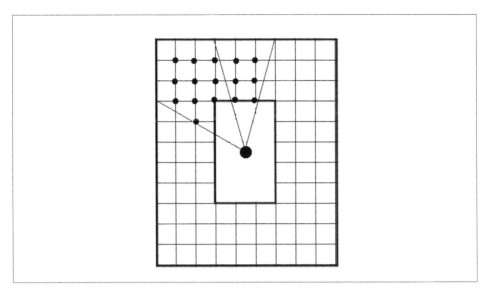

Figure 11-2. If the inner rectangle represents the phone's screen, and the grid intersection indicated potential x and y coordinates, far more enemies will come in from the corner than from straight above

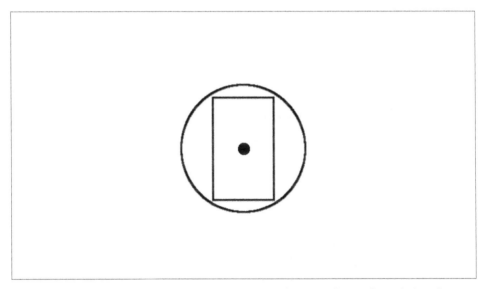

Figure 11-3. Enemies can pop into existence anywhere on the circle and then flow toward the middle

In this case, the enemies will still show up on the screen at different positions, but they won't tend to bunch as they get closer to the middle of the screen. The question, now, is how to do this?[2]

This could be done with some basic trigonometry, but it's easier to let Kivy do the calculating for us. I get anxious when my code includes a lot of calls to cos and sin, partially because it's computationally expensive, but mostly because it's hard to read.

Imagine a clock that has only one hand. The length of the hand is fixed, but it can be rotated to any angle on the clock's face. If you were to choose one of those angles at random, you could place the enemy on the circle at that location. As an added bonus, you'd also know that the direction the enemy must move is along the line to the center of the circle.

The Kivy Vector class gives us this functionality. It is basically a tuple of two values with operators and methods for manipulating combinations of those values. The Vector class can be useful for describing both relative positions and velocities (though not both at the same time). You'll be using vectors as velocities shortly, but let's start with positions.

Vectors, Positions, and Velocities

If, like me, Euclidean geometry and basic physics are but a faded memory of a high-school class that may or may not have been enjoyable, you have a couple choices. You could try to puzzle through the Wikipedia entries on Euclidean vectors, position vectors, and velocity, or you could tell yourself a few lies about their definitions that are close enough to the truth to define the physics in this game.

Vectors are the first lie. You don't need the linear algebra textbook definition of a vector. Simply think of a vector of two x and y values. They don't have to mean much more than this until you start thinking of the relationship between two vectors.

A position is two x and y values (therefore, a vector), such that those values represent a position relative to some origin. If x and y are both zero, then the position is at the origin. You can calculate the length of the vector, which is the distance between the position and the origin. If you have two position vectors, you can calculate the distance between them or the angle between them as though you were to draw lines from those two positions to the origin. Most of the methods on the Vector class are most easily interpreted as though it represented a position vector.

Technically, a velocity is the rate of change of a position. More comprehensibly, it represents both the direction that the position is moving and the amount of distance the position will move in a given unit of time. This can also be represented as a vector (an x and y coordinate), but instead of thinking of those two numbers as a position, you can

---

2. The short answer is: pay attention during math and physics classes in high school.

think of them as the amount of x and amount of y that will be added to that position in the next second. Then each second, the position will move vector.length units in the direction the vector defines.

Going back to the idea of placing the enemies at a random point on a circle outside the screen, the first question is how big the circle should be. Starting at the center of the screen, the furthest away a point can be and still be visible is any of the four corners of the screen. So make the radius of the circle equivalent to the distance to a corner of the screen. The corner can be suitably represented as a position vector, where the origin is in the center of the screen. Then the x and y positions of the corner are half the width and height of the screen.

Once you have defined this vector, you can use the rotate function to rotate it through a randomly chosen angle (in degrees). This is covered in one line of code in Example 11-4.

Remember that the enemy class has a velocity as well as a position. This covers both the direction the enemy is moving and the amount of distance it moves in that direction each second. Because you want the enemy moving toward the middle of the screen (which is the origin of the position above), the direction can be calculated from the position you just derived.

"Wait, what?" you ask. That's right. I'm suddenly switching from thinking of that vector as a position to thinking of it as a velocity. The x and y coordinates of that position can just as easily represent the amount of distance an entity is moving in one second. If you multiply the vector by -1, you can create a velocity that says, "Move this position to the center of the screen in one second".

Of course, that would be moving the enemy way too fast. You need to give your user a bit of a chance, or she isn't going to want to play the game. Luckily, you can call the normalize() method on the vector, which essentially converts the vector to one that is moving in the same direction but has a length of only one unit (units can be anything, but I'm using display pixels). That means the velocity would be one display pixel per second. Unfortunately, that's far too slow. You have to make the game interesting or the user isn't going to want to play the game at all. Thus, you can multiply this unit rate of motion by 50dp (I made that up using trial and error; feel free to toy with it) to make it move at a reasonable rate.

Hopefully that extremely long explanation in English made enough sense to see how the rather short new lines of code in Example 11-4 instantiate an enemy with an appropriate position and direction.

Example 11-4. Using a random vector to place new enemies.

```
def make_enemy(self, delta):
    pos = Vector(self.root.center).rotate(random.randint(0, 360))   ❶
    direction = (-1 * pos).normalize() * dp(50)   ❷
    enemy = Enemy()   ❸
    enemy.pos = pos + self.root.center - Vector(enemy.size) / 2   ❹
    enemy.direction = direction
    self.root.add_widget(enemy)
    self.schedule_next_enemy()
```

❶ You'll need to run `from kivy.vector import Vector` at the top of the file. I cheated and created a `Vector` from the lower-left corner of the screen to the center of the screen using `self.root.center`. This is mathematically equivalent to creating a `Vector` from an origin at the center of the screen to the upper-left corner. This vector is then rotated through a random angle.

❷ Multiplying a vector by `-1` means that its x and y position are both negated, effectively switching the direction of the vector. Normalizing it and multiplying by 50 display pixels makes all the enemies move toward the center at the same time.

❸ I constructed an empty `Enemy` and set the position and direction as separate statements because I wanted access to the size (as set in the *energy.kv* file) in the position calculation.

❹ The coolest thing about the `Vector` class is how easily you can combine it with other vectors or tuples mathematically. This code first adds `self.root.center` to the `pos`, which effectively shifts the origin to the lower-left corner, which is the coordinate system used for positioning widgets. Then it subtracts a new vector that is first constructed from the `size` of the widget and then divided by two. This effectively shifts the enemy's position so that the center of the enemy is on the imaginary circle instead of the lower-left corner.

If you run this code, you won't really see any enemies show up on the screen (except in the corners), since the circle they are appearing on are all outside the window. However, for testing, you can change the position assignment line to `pos = (Vector(self.root.center) / 10).rotate(random.randint(0, 360))` (the center vector is divided by 10)[3]. If you do this and let it run long enough, you will end up with a circle of enemies suspended around the main character, unable to move any closer. This effect is shown in Figure 11-4.

---

3. If I had not done this, I would not have noticed that my circle was off-center when I subtracted the entire `size` instead of dividing it by two in Example 11-4

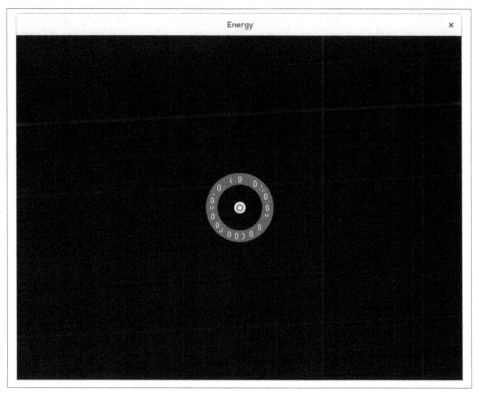

Figure 11-4. Enemies pop up in a circle around the main character.

Updating Enemy Position and Managing Their Score

Having a position and vector, it is almost too easy to add an update method to the Enemy
class that moves the enemies an appropriate amount on scheduled clock intervals. See
Example 11-5.

Example 11-5. Moving enemies about

```
class Enemy(FloatLayout):
    score = NumericProperty(0)
    velocity = ListProperty([0, 0])

    def __init__(self, **kwargs):
        super(Enemy, self).__init__(**kwargs)
        Clock.schedule_interval(self.update, 0.03)

    def update(self, delta):
        self.pos = Vector(self.pos) + Vector(self.direction) * delta
```

Running this code will show the enemies on the move, each one passing right through the character in the center like a neutrino. The scores for all enemies are zero, no matter what their distance to the center is, and there is zero interaction with the main ship (either the enemy or the ship should die when they touch), but at least they are moving. Let's fix those two oversights next.

The number of points you can get for killing an enemy is directly derived from how far it is from the center of the window (this encourages the player to expend energy growing the ship.) The maximum score is five and amounts to one point for every 50 display pixels the enemy is from the center of the screen. This calculation is shown in Example 11-6, along with a minor refactor to reuse the vector created from pos.

Example 11-6. Incrementing the enemy score

```
def update(self, delta):
    app = App.get_running_app()
    pos = Vector(self.pos)
    self.pos = pos + Vector(self.direction) * delta
    self.score = min(5, int(pos.distance(app.root.center) / 50) + 1)
```

Since the enemy's label is updated each time the score changes, nothing needs to change in the KV language file. If you run this version of the code for a while, you'll see enemies moving across the screen with the scores decrementing as they approach the center and incrementing as they leave. I can't capture the motion, but the screenshot in Figure 11-5 should be a small indication.

Updating the Score

Each time the enemy's position is updated, you can also check to see if it has touched the ship itself, and if so, either remove the enemy and increment the app's score, or end the game, depending on whether the ship was safe or not. In order to do this, you'll need access to the Ship class from inside the Enemy class. There are a few ways to do this, but the one that seems most future friendly is to make the ship accessible as an ObjectProp erty on the app itself. Add ObjectProperty to the imports and add the property, as shown in Example 11-7.

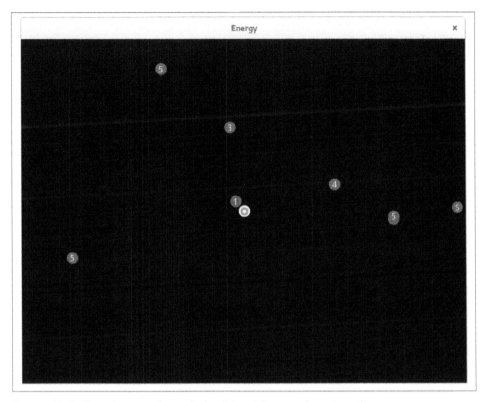

Figure 11-5. Enemies pass through the ship with scores based on distance

Example 11-7. Adding an ObjectProperty

```
class EnergyApp(App):
    enemy_rate = NumericProperty(5)
    score = NumericProperty(0)
    ship = ObjectProperty()
```

The new `ship` property can be set when the `Ship` class is constructed, as shown in Example 11-8.

Example 11-8. Setting the ObjectProperty

```
    def __init__(self, **kwargs):
        super(Ship, self).__init__(**kwargs)
        Clock.schedule_interval(self.update, 0.03)
        App.get_running_app().ship = self
```

With that little bit of data shuffling out of the way, the math to increment the score in the `Enemy`'s update method follows nicely. See the discussion in Example 11-9.

Example 11-9. Updating the score

```
if app.ship:
    if (
        (Vector(self.center) - app.root.center).length()   ❶
        <
        (self.width + app.ship.width) / 2   ❷
    ):
        if app.ship.growth > 0:   ❸
            Clock.unschedule(self.update)   ❹
            self.parent.remove_widget(self)   ❺
            app.score += self.score
            print("CURRENT SCORE: %s" % app.score)
        else:
            app.root.remove_widget(app.ship)   ❻
            app.ship = ""
            print("GAME OVER")
            print("FINAL SCORE: %s" % app.score)
```

❶   If the distance between the center of the dot and the center of the ship …

❷   is less than half the width of the ship plus half the width of the dot …

❸   then the enemy is touching the ship and someone must die. If the ship is currently growing, then it is safe …

❹   and the enemy must stop moving …

❺   and disappear from the screen, incrementing the score (for now, just print the score to the console, since we don't have a reporting facility yet).

❻   If the ship wasn't safe, remove the ship from the screen and stop interaction, leaving the enemies moving across the screen unfettered.

Reporting the Score

You've now written the playable components of the game. The last step for this chapter is to render the current score on the screen. This can be done entirely in the *energy.kv* file. All you need to do is add a label to render the score, as shown in Example 11-10.

Example 11-10. A score label that renders the current score

```
FloatLayout:
    Ship:
    ScoreLabel:

<ScoreLabel@Label>:
    font_size: "80dp"
    color: 0.8, 1, 0.8, 0.6
    text: str(app.score)
    size_hint: None, None
    size: self.texture_size
    pos_hint:
```

```
{
"center_x": 0.5,
"center_y": 0.8
}
```

You can format and position the label however you like. I chose to give it a transparent color so you can see the enemies pass beneath it on their way to attack the doomed ship. The end result is rendered in Figure 11-6.

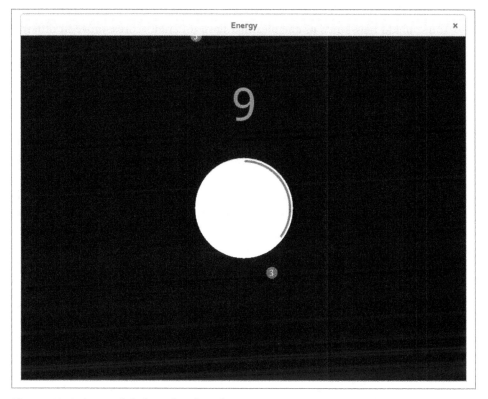

Figure 11-6. A score label rendered on the screen

File It All Away

In this chapter, you've changed your growing, energetic dot into a defensive, vicious growing, energetic dot. Enemies are constantly trying to attack it, and you have a playable game trying to outwit and destroy those enemies while conserving your own score.

This is a very basic game engine, and there are a myriad of ways that you can enhance it. Here are just a few suggestions that you can use to enhance both the game and your understanding of Kivy game design:

- Tweak the various rates in the game. This is a pretty simple game, yet there are quite a few numbers at play. The rate of size growth and energy growth, the speed of the enemies, and the rate at which they appear on the screen can all be tweaked to make the game more playable.

- You can even change these rates dynamically as the game progresses. For example, when the user breaks certain levels, you can make enemies appear on the screen more quickly, or make them start moving faster. Or you could have the ship slowly deteriorate, meaning that its energy recovery speed slows down over time.

- You can add new kinds of enemies that have different scores, move in different paths, obtain different speeds or accelerations, and more. Definitely look into object oriented programming for this; the Enemy class is begging to be subclassed for this purpose.

- You can even add "positive enemies," or powerups, that have a positive effect on your ship when you bump into them.

- The game does not do a very good job of indicating that the game is over. The ship simply disappears. It would be better to tell the user she did a good job and make it easy for her to start a new game.

- This game involves quite a bit of math that translates widget positions to be relative to the center of the screen. That math might be simpler if you were to make judicious use of Kivy's RelativeLayout class instead of FloatLayout.

In the next chapter, you'll add graphics to make the game really come alive.

## CHAPTER 12

Advanced Graphics

The game is pretty functional and playable right now, especially if you improved it according to the suggestions at the end of the last chapter. However, it is rather ugly and boring to look at. Since I'll be designing the graphics for this chapter, I can't promise that it will become less ugly, but I'm pretty sure this chapter will make the game more lively.

A Starfield Background

Start by jazzing up the background. Since this is a space game, a starfield background seems appropriate. The Internet is an amazing resource; I found a terrific GIMP tutorial (*http://bit.ly/gimp-star*) that I adapted to create the tileable starfield in Figure 12-1. You can create your own (be creative!), or download mine from the examples on Git-Hub (*https://github.com/oreillymedia/creating_apps_in_kivy*). Note that I tripled the scale of my version of the image to make it more visible in the print form of this book. This gives it a rather cartoony look. Create a new folder named *images* in your project folder (at the same level as *main.py* and *energy.kv*). Save the file as *background.png* in that folder.

The next step is to render the image in the app. You could use a Kivy `Image`, but that doesn't give quite the level of control I have in mind. It doesn't easily allow repeating the texture, nor does it facilitate the scrolling animation effect I have in mind.

Instead, create a new subclass of `Widget` in your *main.py* called `ScrollingBackground`. For starters, don't make the background scroll, but just render a static, repeating texture as described in Example 12-1.

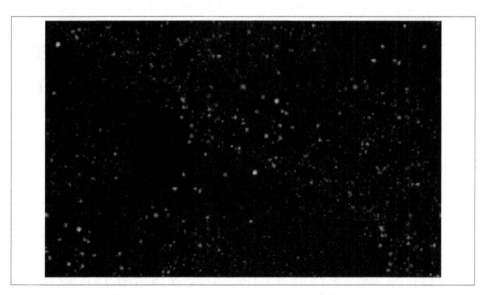

Figure 12-1. A starfield that can scroll across the background.

Example 12-1. A background texture widget

```
class ScrollingBackground(Widget):
    text_rectangle = ObjectProperty()
    def __init__(self, **kwargs):
        super(ScrollingBackground, self).__init__(**kwargs)
        texture = CoreImage("images/background.png").texture    ❶
        texture.wrap = 'repeat'    ❷

        with self.canvas:
            self.text_rectangle = Rectangle(    ❸
                texture=texture,
                size=self.size,
                pos=self.pos
            )
```

❶ You'll need to import `CoreImage` using `from kivy.core.image import Image as CoreImage`. I follow the Kivy developer's example of always renaming this to `CoreImage` when I import it so that it never gets confused with the `kivy.uix.image.Image` class.

❷ Setting `texture.wrap` causes the texture to repeat across whatever size the widget currently has.

❸ You can't do this in KV language, but you can save the `Rectangle` instruction for future manipulation.

Before you can see this code in action, you'll need to add an instance of the new class to the KV language file. Example 12-2 shows how the background widget is added before other widgets in the FloatLayout so that the gameplay widgets show up in front of it.

Example 12-2. Adding a ScrollingBackground widget to the scene.

```
FloatLayout:
    ScrollingBackground:
    Ship:
    ScoreLabel:
```

You're almost there, but if you run it now, the stars only show up in the lower-left corner of the window.[1] They are 100 pixels square, which is the default size for a widget. You might be surprised to discover that setting a size on the widget won't change the size of the rectangle. This is because you constructed, the rectangle inside the ScrollingBackground constructor, and when it is constructed its size is (100, 100). There is no magic binding size changes in the parent to the canvas as would happen if you were defining the code inside the KV language file. Instead, you'll have to bind to on_size yourself as shown in the draft calculations Example 12-3.

Example 12-3. Resizing the texture

```
def on_size(self, object ,size):
    self.text_rectangle.size = size
    x_scale = size[0] / float(self.text_rectangle.texture.size[0])
    y_scale = size[1] / float(self.text_rectangle.texture.size[1])
    self.text_rectangle.tex_coords =[
        0, y_scale,
        x_scale, y_scale,
        x_scale, 0,
        0, 0
    ]
```

The first line is straightforward enough; it just changes the size of the rectangle to match that of the widget. You could leave this method at that, but it would scale the texture to the size of the window. This would look pretty silly on screens with weird aspect ratios or high pixel densities. It would be better to keep the texture at a fixed size and think of resizing the window as revealing more or less of that texture. The texture has been set up to repeat infinitely in the constructor, so it's not possible to reveal too much of it; it'll just start to repeat. You can manipulate the tex_coord field to get this effect, but first you need to understand what tex_coord actually is.

---

1. They are scaled and barely visible, so I didn't include a screenshot.

The `tex_coord` property is comprised of eight separate numbers, which are better thought of as four x, y pairs. Loosely, these numbers correspond to the four corners[2] of the texture, starting (in Kivy) at the upper-left corner and working your way clockwise. These numbers *do not* map to the coordinate space of the input image (i.e., pixels) nor do they map to the coordinate space of the `Rectangle` that is being drawn (i.e., the position and size of the widget). Instead, they represent the percentage of the texture that is attached to the rectangle.

Think of the rectangle as a metal frame to which you are attaching an infinitely stretchy piece of rubber that has had the texture printed on it. You could fasten the rubber to the frame such that its four corners line up exactly. Or you could stretch the rubber so that half the texture is fastened on the frame in one or both dimensions. Or, if your piece of rubber had an infinitely repeating pattern of the texture on it, you could "unstretch" it such that two copies of the texture showed up between the two corners of the frame.

`tex_coord` provides the numbers to facilitate this analogy. By default, the four corners of a single copy of the texture are fastened to the rectangle it is being drawn on. This means 100% of the texture is used in both the x and y dimensions, and the `tex_coord_ values range from +0.0 to 1.0` in both directions. Thus, the default texture coordinates look like Figure 12-2. Since the `tex_coord` list starts in the upper right corner and works clockwise, the list of coordinates is (`0.0, 1.0, 1.0, 1.0, 1.0, 0.0, 0.0, 0.0`).

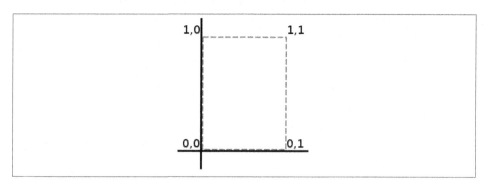

Figure 12-2. Texture coordinates

Now you have enough knowledge to understand the code in Example 12-3. Two variables are set to calculate the scale of the texture independently in each dimension. These numbers would work out to `1.0` (and the `tex_coord` would stay at its default value) only

---

2. `tex_coord` is actually an OpenGL construct and can have many values in 3D programming where polygons of any size and shape are common. In Kivy, however, almost all your textures will be rectangular, so this discussion focuses on four concrete corners.

---

if the window is exactly the same size as the input texture. Once these values are calculated, the `tex_coord` property is set on the rectangle so that the texture shows up at the appropriate location. The net result is shown in Figure 12-3.

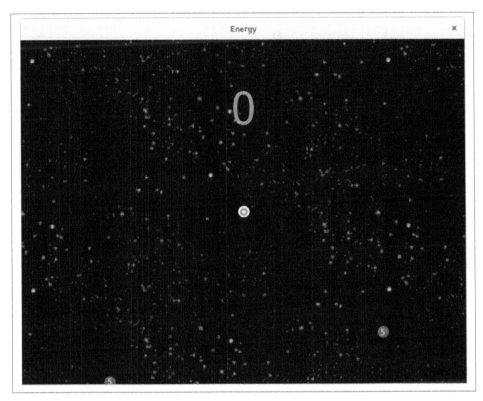

Figure 12-3. Texture coordinates

Scrolling the Background

Having the ship rendered in front of a starry background is certainly nicer than a black box, but it is in the nature of spacecraft to move, and to move quickly, according to sci-fi lore. As you might have guessed from the class name, the next step is to make the background scroll in the y dimension, which will give the impression that the ship is moving against a starry background.

This can also be done by tampering with the `tex_coord`. In fact, you can completely replace the `on_size` method with a new `update` method that is scheduled on the clock like the `Enemy` and `Ship` update methods. The reason you can remove `on_size` is that textures will be recomputed several times per second based on the widget size, so you don't have to respond to size events at the same time. See Example 12-4.

Example 12-4. Scrolling background intervals

```
Clock.schedule_interval(self.update, 0.03)   ❶

def update(self, delta):
    self.text_rectangle.size = self.size   ❷
    t = Clock.get_boottime()   ❸
    y_incr = t * -0.5   ❹
    x_scale = self.size[0] / float(self.text_rectangle.texture.size[0])
    y_scale = self.size[1] / float(self.text_rectangle.texture.size[1])
    self.text_rectangle.tex_coords = [   ❺
        0, y_incr + y_scale,
        x_scale, y_incr + y_scale,
        x_scale, y_incr,
        0, y_incr
    ]
```

❶   This line goes at the end of the `ScrollingBackground.init` method.

❷   You still need to update the size of the widget, since there is no longer a `on_size` method. You could have left only this line in `on_size` if you wanted a small optimization.

❸   I don't know what boo technically means, but `get_boo_time` returns the number of seconds that have passed since the app started. You can use this number as a reliable means to calculate `tex_coord` instead of trying to fiddle with incrementing a bunch of values according to `delta`.

❹   `y_incr` is essentially the percentage the texture should move in a second. The number is negative, so the stars are moving downwards, which gives the illusion that the ship is going forward.

❺   The x values stay the same as in the defunct `on_size` method, since nothing is moving in the x dimension. The y values are adjusted so that the top and bottom of the texture are both shifted by `y_incr`. `y_incr` will be a slightly bigger number each time, but since the texture repeats infinitely, this is not a problem. You don't have to optimize for reusing the same texture since OpenGL is already doing that on Kivy's behalf.

If you run this, it will show the background scrolling by at a pretty fast clip[3]. However, it looks kind of flat. In reality (if space travel becomes a reality), parallax would cause some stars to move faster than others. I think this can be simulated by using the same texture but moving at different speeds and offset in the x dimension to prevent weird alignment issues. This will require a couple new properties defined in Example 12-5 and an update to the calculations as described in Example 12-6.

---

3. I won't waste your time with a screenshot since the still looks exactly the same as Figure 12-3.

Example 12-5. Properties to make scrolling background more generic

```
speed = NumericProperty(0.5)
x_offset = NumericProperty(0)
```

Example 12-6. Allow multispeed offset scrolling

```
def update(self, delta):
    self.text_rectangle.size = self.size
    t = Clock.get_boottime()
    y_incr = t * -1 * self.speed      ❶
    x_scale = self.size[0] / float(self.text_rectangle.texture.size[0])
    y_scale = self.size[1] / float(self.text_rectangle.texture.size[1])
    self.text_rectangle.tex_coords = [
        self.x_offset, y_incr + y_scale,      ❷
        self.x_offset + x_scale, y_incr + y_scale,
        self.x_offset + x_scale, y_incr,
        self.x_offset, y_incr
    ]
```

❶   The speed comes from the property now instead of being hardcoded.

❷   The x_offset is added to all x coordinates to pull a different section of texture in for each layer.

Now, you can define multiple ScrollingBackground objects in *energy.kv*, each with its own speed and offset. See Example 12-7.

Example 12-7. Adding three layers of scrolling

```
FloatLayout:
    ScrollingBackground:
    ScrollingBackground:
        speed: 0.3
        x_offset: 0.27
    ScrollingBackground:
        speed: 0.1
        x_offset: 0.73

    Ship:
    ScoreLabel:
```

The result, according to my girlfriend, looks more like snow than stars. Improving the look is discussed in the exercises.

More Animations

There are numerous ways to do animated widgets in Kivy. In Chapter 12, I introduced you to one of the harder ways: drawing graphics manually using `Canvas` instructions and updating them dynamically based on the Kivy clock. You've seen additional uses of `Clock` callbacks for animating sizes, positions, and other properties in this chapter.

This is actually one of the hardest ways to develop animations in Kivy, but it also gives you complete control. The other animation methods use this same method but take care of much of the boilerplate for you.

To illustrate, think about the growing dot that currently represents our ship. It's definitely not very exciting. It would be easy enough to replace this with a static graphic using the `Image` widget, but static graphics are also boring. An animated graphic would be even cooler.

In fact, it is just as easy to add an animated graphic as it is to add a static graphic. The `Image` class's `source` property can be set to a `gif` image, which supports animations, but is considered rather dated because they can only have 256 colors. Luckily, Kivy also supports using a ZIP of *.png* files, which do not have this restriction, for animations.

So I spent an afternoon playing around in the GIMP to create a rotating saucer look. I ended up with 12 images that rotate through 60 degrees of a circle before symmetry takes over. I also added "lights" that flash on and off as the ship rotates. The twelve images I came up with are shown in Figure 12-4.

To create the animated effect, name each image in an increasing order (I used *ship-01.png* through *ship-12-png*) and then zip them all together using your favorite compression program. You can then add that ZIP file as a `source` to any image to get animation for free. The code in Example 12-8 explains some additional changes you need to make to get this animation working with the ship.

Why 12 Graphics Instead of One Rotating Graphic?

You might be wondering why I chose to make an animation composed of 12 separate images instead of designing a single image and using Kivy animations to rotate it. You make a good point, and you certainly can use the `Rotate` canvas instruction to get this effect.[4]

However, I gained two things by using a collection of images instead. It may not be obvious if you're looking at a black-and-white print version of this book, but the 12 images have blue "lights" that flash on and off as the animation rotates.

---

4. You'll also want to look into the `PushMatrix` and `PopMatrix` instructions.

A more subtle effect is that even though these images are two-dimensional shapes, they have been painted as if they contain lighting. There is a shadow toward the lower right and highlights toward the upper left, as if a light source was coming from that direction. If I were to simply rotate this image, the shadow would also rotate, giving the rather odd effect that the light source was rotating around the image.

I constructed the three-dimensional features of the 12 images independently (using GIMP's Bump Map filter) so that the light source always appears to be coming from the upper left for each separate rotation. If other images are added to the game, they can also be two dimensional, but you should consider the direction of the light source for visual consistency.

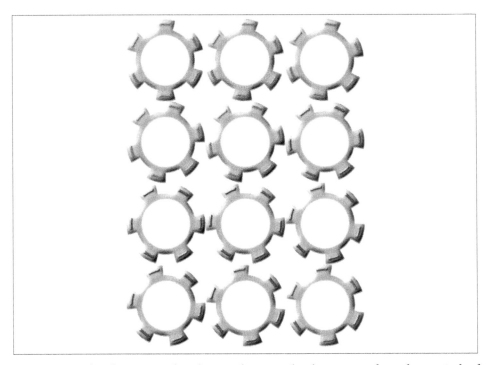

Figure 12-4. If each image replaced its predecessor, the ship rotates through one-sixth of a circle before the pattern repeats

Example 12-8. Animated ZIP ship

```
<Ship>:
    size_hint: None, None
    width: "20dp"
    height: self.width
    pos_hint:
        {
        "center_x": 0.5,
```

```
            "center_y": 0.5
            }
    canvas.after:      ❶
        Color:
            rgba:
                (
                [.3, .4, 1, 1]
                if self.growth > 0 else
                [1, .4, .3, 1]
                )
        Line:
            width: 2
            circle:
                [
                self.center_x,
                self.center_y,
                self.width / 4,    ❷
                360 * self.energy,
                0
                ]
    Image:
        source: "images/ship.zip"    ❸
        anim_delay: 0.05    ❹
        allow_stretch: True    ❺
        size: root.size
        pos: root.pos
```

❶ Since you want the "energy bar" circle to show up in front of the image, apply the instructions to `canvas.after` as discussed in Chapter 12. Also remove the `Color` and `Ellipse` instructions that draw the white circle, since those are now being replaced by an animated image.

❷ This instruction used to place the "energy" arc a fixed width from the edge of the circle. This didn't work with the image version because the image grows as a percentage, and thus the size of the "rim" (for lack of a better word) changes. Dividing the image by four causes the bar to be an approximately consistent distance from the edge.

❸ As discussed in the text, using a ZIP file of images implicitly tells Kivy to create an animation from them.

❹ By default, Kivy will change animation images once per second. Since a full series of animations only rotates the image 1/6 of a revolution, I changed it to change pictures every 0.05 seconds. This gives a fairly steady-looking rate of revolution on the screen.

❺   The `allow_stretch` property tells Kivy to stretch the image to the full size of its widget, rather than trying to center a physical image on the screen. Since this is a circular image on a square size, it will always keep its aspect ratio. If you would like it to stretch unevenly in the horizontal and vertical dimensions, you should also set the `keep_ratio` property to `False`.

Figure 12-5 shows one frame of the animation in progress.

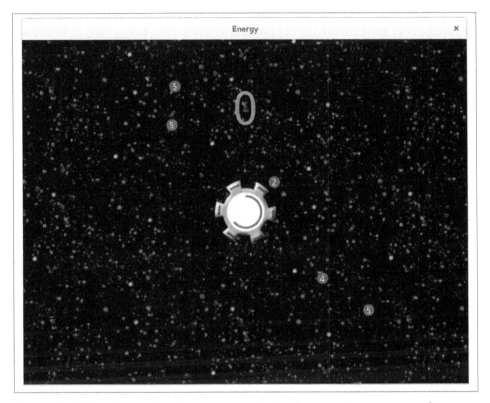

Figure 12-5. The ship rotating (use your imagination) as enemies come toward it

Kivy Atlas

Kivy atlases are a way to collect several static images into a single underlying image and then reference the original images by name. They are strictly a performance speedup; loading a single image and referencing textures from different parts of it is faster than loading several different images into textures. This technique has been used in computer graphics for many generations, most recently in the form of CSS sprites. To demonstrate the use of atlases, I made three images to represent alien spacecraft. I named these three images *enemy-01.png*, *enemy-02.png*, and *enemy-03.png*. The three images are shown together in Figure 12-6.

Figure 12-6. Three enemy ship files

As an exercise, see if you can figure out how to update the Enemy class so that it will choose one of these three image files randomly when it is constructed. That will work just fine, but if you use an atlas, you can get better performance by loading the three textures in a single image file.[5]

To create a kivy atlas, issue the command `python -m kivy.atlas enemies 200 enemy-*.png` (replace `python` with `kivy` on Mac OS) inside the images directory. This command will create two new files: *enemies.atlas* and *enemies.atlas-0.png*.

The `python -m` command tells Python to execute the contents of a module on the path. In this case, that module is `kivy.atlas`. The `kivy.atlas` main program requires a name for the atlas (`enemies` in this case), and the pixel size of each *page* in the atlas. Finally, it accepts the list of images that need to be placed into that atlas.

The atlas program will jam as many of those images as possible into a single page. In this case, all three images fit in one page file *enemies-0.png*. You can open this in a standard editor. It will be a 200 pixel square file that looks like Figure 12-7.

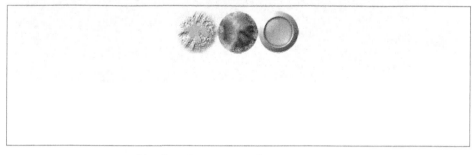

Figure 12-7. Page created by the atlas command

5. Obviously, the performance penalty for three files is not too troubling, but if you wanted to extend this to a lot of images, you would see noticeable improvements, especially on mobile.

The *enemies.atlas* file is a JSON file that describes where in the page each image can be found. You don't really have to know how it is formatted, but it is shown in Example 12-9 for completeness to illustrate how simple an atlas is.

Example 12-9. Atlas file contents

```
{
    "enemies-0.png": {
        "enemy-01": [
            2,
            134,
            64,
            64
        ],
        "enemy-03": [
            134,
            134,
            64,
            64
        ],
        "enemy-02": [
            68,
            134,
            64,
            64
        ]
    }
}
```

Essentially, the atlas says which page each original file is mapped to, as well as what coordinates that image is located at within the file.

Using an Atlas

Once an atlas has been created, it is trivial to use images inside it anywhere you would use a normal image in Kivy. For example, you can replace the canvas instruction in the Enemy KV language style with an image, as shown in Example 12-10. The result is illustrated in Figure 12-8.[6]

Example 12-10. Render an image in the KV language file

```
<Enemy>:
    size_hint: None, None
    width: "20dp"
    height: self.width
    Image:
        source: "atlas://images/enemies/enemy-0%s" % random.randint(1, 3)    ❶
        allow_stretch: True
```

---

6. It took several attempts to get all three enemy images on the screen without dying.

```
    size: root.size
    pos: root.pos
Label:
    pos: root.pos
    size: self.texture_size
    color: 0, 0, 0, 1
    markup: True
    text: "[b]%s[/b]" % str(root.score)   ❷
```

❶ When using an atlas source, the path is *atlas://* followed by the path to the atlas file name without the *.atlas* extension (i.e., *images/enemies*) followed by a / and finally, the name of the file that was inputted into the atlas, without its extension (*enemy-01*). In this case, in order to randomly select one of three files, I imported the random module into the KV language file using the syntax `#:import ran dom random` at the top of the file. Thus, each of the three atlas names might be generated (*enemy-01*, *enemy-02*, and *enemy-03*).

❷ To make the score label a little more readable in front of the image, I changed the color to black, enabled the `markup` attribute, and used the Kivy markup syntax (not unlike bbcode) to make the label bold.

Animating Properties

Take a step back from graphics for a bit and think about another way to animate things. You are already doing some animations in this code that do not involve changing graphics. The ship, for example, has an animated size; it shrinks and grows depending on user input. Enemies also have animation; their position changes as they move toward the ship.

For these animations, it makes sense to do the calculations manually inside the up date methods because they are dependent on a few variables, like whether the user is touching the screen and what the current size of the ship is. However, for simpler work that is dependent only on time, you can use the `Animation` class. To illustrate this, I'm going to change the size of the score label each time the player scores points. It's going to grow to a specific size and then shrink back down to its original size. To make it more interesting, it's also going to "bounce" a bit as it approaches its original size. Kivy animations can take care of this transition for you, as you can see in Example 12-11.

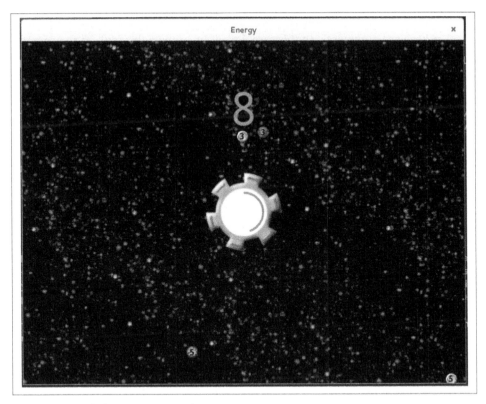

Figure 12-8. All three images on the screen

Example 12-11. Animations on the score font size

```
if app.ship.growth > 0:
    Clock.unschedule(self.update)
    self.parent.remove_widget(self)
    app.score += self.score
    anim = Animation(       ❶
        font_size=dp(140),  ❷
        duration=0.3,       ❸

        ) + Animation(      ❹
        font_size=dp(80),
        duration=1.0,
        t="out_bounce"      ❺
        )
    anim.start(app.root.score_label)  ❻
```

❶   You'll need to from kivy.animation import Animation. This constructs an animation object.

❷   You can specify any numeric property, or combination of numeric properties, as keyword arguments. In this case, I want to animate the `font_size` property, so I tell the animation what the desired end size is.

❸   The duration of the animation in seconds. At the end of 0.3 seconds, the `font_size` will have grown from its default 80 display pixels to to 140 display pixels. The default transition is linear, so it will grow smoothly.

❹   Animations can be combined using the + operator. This essentially says that after the animation completes, another one will start immediately. You can also combine animations in parallel using the & operator.

❺   This animation brings the size back down to 80 display pixels. However, it's using a bounce transition, so instead of shrinking directly, it will approach that size, then grow a bit and shrink some more.

❻   Animations are created independently of the widgets they run on. That way you can use the same animation effect on different widgets for different reasons. In this case, you are applying the animation to the `score_label`, which you can make accessible as shown in Example 12-12.

Example 12-12. Making score_label property accessible

```
FloatLayout:
    score_label: score_label    ❶
    ScrollingBackground:
    ScrollingBackground:
        speed: 0.3
        x_offset: 0.27
    ScrollingBackground:
        speed: 0.1
        x_offset: 0.73

    Ship:
    ScoreLabel:
        id: score_label    ❷
```

❶   As you've seen before, you can create an `ObjectProperty` dynamically without defining it in the Python class. This puts a `score_label` property on the root widget and sets it to the widget with an ID of the same name.

❷   Here's where the ID is set. Now you can access that widget as `app.root.score_la bel` in the code, as you saw in Example 12-11.

File It All Away

This chapter completed the game you've been working on with pretty animations and graphics. You used several different animation techniques to create a layered scrolling background, a rotating space ship, colored enemies, and even an animated score label. This game has a lot of potential, and there are a lot of things you can look into to make it better. Here are a bunch of topics you might want to cover to really get into Kivy:

- Can you work out how to flip a texture in one or both dimensions using just `tex_coord`?
- In the scrolling backgrounds, figure out how to make the textures that are farther back (slower) have darker backgrounds.
- I briefly introduced the label markup syntax here; look at the Kivy documentation to see other things you can do with markup syntax.
- Play around with animating different numeric properties such as size, position, and transparency. Also toy with the different transitions discussed in the Kivy documentation. If you are feeling ambitious, try making your own transition.
- I had originally intended to cover sound in this chapter, but it went a little over the intended length. Kivy provides a very simple sound API; try playing a sound each time the user scores.
- Create a Buildozer environment and deploy your game to your mobile device.

That's all for this book! I've really enjoyed writing it, and I hope you have encountered even more joy in the reading. You should now have a pretty good idea as to the many things you can do with Kivy; I hope you'll be submitting your own Kivy apps to the various mobile markets soon!

Index

A
absolute positioning, 121
absolute sizes, 14, 122
ActionBar widget, 101
adb logcat, 112
AddLocationForm widget
    adding logic to, 23
    adding properties to, 25
    args_converter method on, 50
    creating, 12
    improving, 46
    normal vs. dynamic class, 22
    rendering of, 13
    root widget with AddLocationForm child, 35
    setting size of, 17
    updating search results, 30
    viewing with ModalView.open(), 97
Android Debug Bridge (adb), 112
Android devices
    deployment to, 2, 106
    GPS access, 115
    lack of menu key on, 81
animation
    basic, 67
    using .png files, 156
    using Carousel, 96
    using properties, 162
APIs
    choosing, 27
    Kivy documentation, 18
App objects, 5
app.root, 40
Apple Developer Account, 113
Apple's XCode, 87, 113
application, examples of basic/less basic, 5-6
args_converter, 50
AsyncImage widget, 70
automatic property assignment, 76

B
backgrounds, 149
    (see also graphics)
Balsamiq (mockup creator), 9
BoxLayout subclass, 10
Buildozer
    Android build specifications, 107
    benefits/drawbacks of, 105
    debugging Android deployment, 111
    diagnostic information, 112
    downloading, 105
    iOS specification, 114
    Python support, 107
buttons
    Add Location button, 43
    adjusting size of, 13
    back button, 101
    Button widget, 10
    cancel button, 47, 99

We'd like to hear your suggestions for improving our indexes. Send email to index@oreilly.com.

connecting event handlers to, 24
creating custom widgets for, 12
Current Location button, 32
in UI design, 9
Search button, 28, 46
setting menu, 81
styling multiple, 22
switching views with, 83
tracking selection of, 36

C

C library dependencies, 4
caching, 47
cancel button, 47, 99
canvas property, 60
Carousel widget, 96
celsius, 80
circle parameter, 131
circular gesture, 87
classes
    dynamic, 22
    making dynamic classes static, 54
    of ActionBar, 101
    Python vs. dynamic, 41
client libraries, choosing, 27
Clock.schedule… construct, 136
code refactoring
    drawbacks of, 65
    importance of, 53
    improving usability with, 95
    to do list for, 99
code smells, 48
comprehensions, 29
conditions widget, 59
configuration settings, 77
container widgets, 41
country codes, 49
cross-platform deployment, 115
CurrentWeather widget, 96

D

data
    dictionary storage of, 50
    public sources for, 27
    storing local, 73
debugging
    advanced widgets and, 95
    Android Debug Bridge (adb), 112

Android deployment, 111
in Buildozer, 105
in Mac OS installations, 3
Internet Relay Chat (IRC), 112
Kivy Remote Shell, 112
syntax errors, 11
    (see also warnings/errors)
timing of, 41
USB Debugging, 111
viewing logging output, 114
dependencies
    Buildozer on Mac OS, 114
    C library, 4
    challenges of, 2
    during deployment, 105
    Kivy.app bundle, 4
deployment
    Android devices, 106
    Buildozer benefits/drawbacks, 105
    Buildozer download, 105
    cross-platform, 115
    iOS devices, 87, 113
developer options, unlocking, 111
DictAdapter class, 50
dictionary comprehensions, 29
display pixels, 127
displays
    adapting to current, 10
    display pixels, 17
    KV language file and, 22
    popup windows, 97
    reusing layout settings, 22
    setting proportions, 13
    switching between, 96
duplicate code, 65
dynamic classes, 22

E

editors, 5
energy
    displaying, 130
    options for rendering, 127, 130
    recording, 129
errors (see warnings/errors)
event handlers
    adding to KV language file, 24
    attaching, 91
    basics of, 21
    cancel button, 99

pause mode, 117
Pencil (mockup creator), 9
pixels, display vs. real, 127
placeholders, 40
plyer API, 115
Popup widget, 97
positional arguments, 76, 140
program editors, 5
programming workflow
    code refactoring, 53, 95
    dependency management, 114
    duplicate code, 65
    iterative development, 45
properties
    accessing in KV language widgets, 25
    animating, 162
    automatic assignment of, 76
    basics of, 25
    Kivy vs. Python, 26
proportions, setting, 13
public data sources, 27
put keyword, 76
pyjnius library, 115
pyobjus library, 115
Python
    Buildozer support, 107
    class vs. dynamic widgets, 41
    comprehensions in, 29
    creating a label in, 40
    editors for, 5
    imports in, 36
    list.clear() in, 39
    properties in, 26
    storage modules available, 73
    super keyword in, 70
    tracebacks, 112
    version selection, 2
Python-to-Java (pyjnius) bridge, 112

Q

quick installers, 3

R

Raspberry Pi, 113
real pixels, 127
refactoring
    drawbacks of, 65
    importance of, 53

improving usability with, 95
    to do list for, 99
root magic variable, 40
root widgets, 10, 35
rotate function, 141
run method, 21

S

ScrollingBackground widget, 151
Scrum, 45
search input widget, 25
search result list, populating, 27
set comprehensions, 29
size hints, 14
snow animation, 67
starfield background
    creating, 149
    scrolling, 153
storage
    key/value storage, 73
    maintaining location list, 73
    of location list, 75
    options available, 73
    user setting dialog, 77
Sublime Text, 5
sunshine graphic, 63
super keyword, 70
swappable widgets, 41
syntax errors, 11

T

TabbedPanel widget, 10
tabs, adding, 73, 83
temperature system setting, 80
text
    displaying with Label widget, 10
    editors for, 5
TextInput widget, 10, 46
tex_coord property, 152
touch events, 89
transformations, 29
tuples, 50
type checking, 25

U

UI (user interface), design of, 8
UnknownConditions widget, 59

About the Author

Dusty Phillips is a Canadian software engineer and author. He holds a master's degree in computer science and is an active member of various open source communities, most notably Python, Arch Linux, and Gittip. He has written two previous books and won the 2010 Django Dash.

Colophon

The animal on the cover of *Creating Apps in Kivy* is a kiang (*Equus kiang*). Native to the Tibetan plateau, the kiang is the largest of all wild asses and has never been domesticated. They bear a resemblance to donkeys and mules, although they are generally brown and tan as opposed to gray.

Adult kiangs can reach 13.3 hands (or 55 inches) tall at the shoulder and weigh around 900 pounds. They have large heads with convex muzzles and short, upright manes. A dark brown dorsal stripe reaches from the mane to the tail, a feature that can be found on many varieties of wild ass.

The kiang's Tibetan habitat is mostly alpine meadows and steppe country, where there is plenty of grass and shrubbery for grazing. The only predators the kiang faces, aside from humans, are wolves. The first response of a kiang is to flee from danger, but they will also use their powerful kick to deter an attacker if necessary.

Sometimes kiangs gather together in large herds, but most of the time they are separated into smaller groups. Older males have harems of females that can grow to almost 50 members. Each stallion controls an area of about two square miles, and vicious fights often occur when a younger male challenges a stallion's supremacy.

Although population numbers have declined in recent years due to encroaching human territory and having to share grazing space with farmers' herds, the kiang is still considered a common sight and is not listed as threatened or endangered. In 1950, Thubten Jigme Norbu, the elder brother of the 14th Dalai Lama, was traveling through northern China and observed a herd of kiang moving across the plateau. He wrote, "They look wonderfully graceful and elegant when you see them darting across the steppes like arrows, heads stretched out and tails streaming away behind them in the wind."

The cover image is from Cassell's *Natural History*. The cover fonts are URW Typewriter and Guardian Sans. The text font is Adobe Minion Pro; the heading font is Adobe Myriad Condensed; and the code font is Dalton Maag's Ubuntu Mono.

Have it your way.

Lightning Source UK Ltd.
Milton Keynes UK
UKOW07f1952180917
309420UK00001B/5/P

9 781491 946671